DAVID'S STORY

A CASUALTY OF VIETNAM

Center For The Advancement Of Human Dignity
Vietnam Veterans Chapel
Springer, New Mexico

DAVID'S STORY

A CASUALTY OF VIETNAM

Victor Westphall

CENTER
For The Advancement
Of Human Dignity


VIETNAM VETERANS CHAPEL

FOR ALL VIETNAM VETERANS

wherever they may be;
the living, the dead, and
the maimed in body and spirit.

# ACKNOWLEDGMENTS

I am particularly indebted to Betty Fleissner who named DAVID'S STORY and encouraged me to write the book.

The contributions of Major Rocky Wirsching and 1st Sergeant Tom McKinney were especially valuable to the chapters on Vietnam. Their written recollections competently supplemented David's letters from Vietnam. I used them often literally and without direct attribution in these chapters, but make that ascription here instead.

I must acknowledge my own instinct for saving the letters and memorabilia that made DAVID'S STORY possible. These included my wife's letters to me while I was overseas in World War II, and David's letters written throughout his lifetime.

I am grateful to Rocky Wirsching, Tom McKinney, Pete McDavid, Betty Fleissner, and Don Borgeson who read portions of the manuscript and made suggestions for the improvement of various chapters.

My special thanks goes to my wife Jeanne, and son, Douglas, who gave constant encouragement, and to Juanita Montoya who typed the manuscript.

V.W.

# INTRODUCTION

People who have known that I was writing a book about my son who was killed in Vietnam have not generally expressed to me a recognition of the lonely agony of calling to mind bitter memories day after interminable day in the way that is necessary in fashioning a lengthy narrative.

This lack of recognition brings home with stark reality the truism that life is for the living, and that memories of the dead are too often cast upon the rubbish heap of things past and done.

The fact is that while David's life was entirely noteworthy in its own right, I would surely not have written of it had he not been a deceased Vietnam veteran. So in a very real sense this book represents all Vietnam veterans: "The living, the dead, and the maimed in body and spirit."

Their voices cry out from the grave, from hospitals where they lie crippled for life, from the gutters where they have fallen because a callous society has rejected them, from every segment of society, tolling an uncoordinated and dispirited message that should be heard everywhere.

They say to us in feeble tones that should be amplified into rolling and thundering cadences: "Wake up you people of Planet Earth. You forget the lessons of Vietnam at your peril." They add: "Is it not obvious to every thinking being that we can no longer afford to waste our precious resources on the expensive frivolity of war?"

If it were not for the chronological juxtaposition of the Vietnam War with this era of rapid depletion of nature's legacy, perhaps that war could be considered just another unfortunate conflict. As it is, though, one Vietnam veteran characterized its significance cogently when he spoke up boldly for his buddies. He said: "God visited this horribly stupid conflict upon us to warn us of the imminent danger of our time."

I could not have written about my son's experiences and death in Vietnam without steeling myself into an almost trance-like objectivity. I could not have set down this account of war as war is fought while loathing it as I do had I not been able to follow it up with the positive message of the Vietnam Veterans Peace and Brotherhood Chapel.

I feel that this message is worthy of admission to the most inclusive mores of American society. No matter that it is almost solely the product of one bereaved father who would not, could not, forget the tragic and lonely travail of Vietnam veterans as they struggle for a cohesive voice to present their warning before the forum of the spirit of America. Surely that divine essence has not irretrievably lost the sense of superior values that marked this country's rise to greatness.

# GLOSSARY

AK-47:  Russian made assault rifle
ARVN:  Army of the Republic of Vietnam
Chopper:  Helicopter
CO:  Commanding Officer
CP:  Command Post
DMZ:  Demilitarized Zone
FO:  Forward Observer
Gook:  American slang term for Asian person
Grunt:  GI slang for infantryman
H&I:  Harassment and Interdiction
Helo:  Helicopter
Hootch:  Vietnamese hut, also structures built by Americans
        as living quarters
HQ:  Headquarters
LZ:  Landing Zone
MACV:  Military Assistance Command Vietnam
Medevac:  Medical Evacuation
mm:  millimeter
MOS:  Military Occupational Specialty
NCO:  Non-commissioned Officer
NVA:  North Vietnamese Army
OP:  Observation Post
OTS:  Officer Training School
R&R:  Rest and Recreation, or Rest and Recuperation
RPG:  Russian made rocket-propelled grenade
Satchel Charge:  Hand carried demolition charge
Seabee:  Navy Construction Battalion
Tubing:  Incoming artillery or mortar fire
USAID:  US Agency for International Development
VC:  Vietcong
Ville:  Village
XO:  Executive Officer

# PROLOGUE

On the afternoon of May 27, 1968, I was operating a backhoe in pursuance of developing our mountain recreational subdivision at Val Verde Ranch in the Moreno Valley near Eagle Nest in northern New Mexico. I had just set up near the bottom of a steep slope overlooking the nearby entrance road. The high operator's seat provided a clear view of the road; however, efficient operation of a backhoe demands close concentration so I did not see an automobile approach bearing two Marine Corps captains until the vehicle had stopped and its occupants had hurried almost upon me. They had come many miles bearing a pitiless message that they dreaded to deliver, but duty compelled them to hasten toward the completion of their grim task.

The leader asked: "Are you Doctor Westphall?"

I replied affirmatively, already feeling a numbing apprehension.

The tidings they bore could not be softened by sympathetic preparatory words so before my attention could shift to possible reasons for the presence before me of uniformed visitors, the inexorable words rose up to me: "Your son has been killed."

Our son—our first-born—28-year-old 1st Lieutenant Victor David Westphall III, U.S.M.C.

I heard, but for long moments I could not, would not, comprehend. The newcomers before me, the awful moment of their visitation now complete, were all compassion and twice offered to help me down.

I declined their considerate overture and laboriously dismounted from my high perch. As my feet touched earth a single piteous word hesitantly and tenderly escaped me, expressing a question that conveyed faint hope as well as a request for confirmation and identity.

"David?"

Both officers glanced up sharply. For a fleeting moment that seemed like eternity it appeared that there might have been a mistake. But the answer came quickly.

"Victor."

The glimmer of hope was gone. Our son's name was Victor David, but we called him David just as we called our younger son and only other child, Douglas, although his name was Walter Douglas. Victor and Walter were my first and middle names.

The half-mile ride to our home was marked by hesitant verbal sparring as though to somehow turn back the clock of time past the brutal moment that was the cause of our brief journey. How could I tell my wife, Jeanne? What could I possibly say that would be merciful? When we reached the house, my compassionate attendants asked if they should go in with me. I replied: "No, let me go in alone."

I struggled rigorously with my thoughts as I approached the door. In the end I could think of no more appropriate statement than a paraphrase of that offered by my informants. I said as sympathetically as I could: "David has been killed."

My wife was stunned nearly to insensibility, but quickly controlled her grief as her thoughts turned to Douglas who was in the final weeks of college in preparation for O.T.S. and a commission in the Air Force. She thought of his love and admiration for his older brother, and how hard the tidings would be for him to bear during his last crucial weeks of college. We agreed, however, that he must be told promptly.

In my call to him, and in numerous others to relatives and friends that followed, I could think of no better dialogue than the razor-sharp litany that cut clean and quick: "David has been killed." Douglas' first words were: "Oh, no," uttered in a tone of mortal anguish that lacerated my soul to the well-spring of my being. Dear David, dear brother David, was gone. Perhaps this unhappy tiding was harder for him than all the rest of us to bear. His long and lonely flight home was marked by searing mental torment.

The bearers of the grievous message, both Vietnam combat veterans, had borne similar ones to other next-of-kin and let us know unequivocally that this was the hardest duty they had ever been called upon to perform. Practice had taught them that the kindest thing for them to do was excuse themselves as soon as they were reasonably sure that they had rendered every possible assistance. With an admonition to keep in touch with them for any other help they could give, they were gone.

In their search for us they had inquired of neighbors as to the location of our home, and word of our bereavement soon spread through the valley. We were relative newcomers there and had not made many friends, but found that we had more of them than we knew. They appeared throughout the afternoon and evening with food and quiet words of sympathy and condolence. We appreciated these cordial calls as one is wont to do in such circumstances, yet it was a relief to finally be alone so that we could sort out the bits and pieces of this cruel twist in our lives.

David's brief sojourn through life had been accompanied by more than his share of affronts to his sensitive nature. Thus it was that the thought came to me over and over again: "No one can ever hurt him again. He has been through his agony with the callousness of his fellow men, and has found his place and his peace." I tried to solace my wife with this idea, but she was wounded deeper than I knew.

I was in the consequential process of piping water to golf course putting greens, and the strenuous physical exertion involved was therapy of a sort. Jeanne had no comparable buttress against emotional shock, so the interminable time of waiting for details and clarifications was harder on her than for myself.

The customary formal telegram arrived the following day, and informed us only that David had died on May 22 in the vicinity of Quang Tri, Republic of Vietnam. Reportedly, "He sustained a gunshot wound to the body from hostile rifle fire while engaged in action against hostile forces." We now already had variant information, for the Marine Corps emissaries of the day before had heard—although they could not vouch for the authenticity of their information—that he had been killed by a rocket.

The telegram had promised that a letter would follow. This message did come and was dated May 31, 1968: it was from Lieutenant Colonel J. H. MacLean, newly appointed Commander, 1st Battalion, 4th Marines (Rein) 3d Marine Division (Rein) FMF. In it was the unbelievably naive assertion that David had died from gun shot wounds to both arms and legs. Gun shot wounds to both arms and legs were cer-

3

tainly not even reasonably compatible with instant death, a fact which Douglas, hesitating just short of bitter wrath, pointed out immediately after he read the letter. Nor was it consistent with the later development that his remains were not viewable.

It would be a year-and-a-half before we began to learn the facts in a letter of December 24, 1970, from Thomas F. McKinney, 1st Sergeant of Bravo Company, who was in the ambush in which David lost his life. Sergeant McKinney wrote that in all between 5:20 and 5:40 on the afternoon of May 22, 1968, Bravo Company lost 13 dead and 27 wounded. These included every officer, radio man, and all but two Staff noncom's, including himself. He provided additional information later.

Sergeant McKinney's account was confirmed in detail a few days later by Captain William Jason Spangler, who assumed command of Company B. the morning after the ambush. He called me from Red River ski area the last evening of 1970, and I gave him and his party a ski lesson on New Year's Day.

He related that David's platoon was providing security for the headquarters group when it was fired upon from ambush. When all its officers and radio men were killed, the sector started to give way. David left his platoon in charge of his sergeant (who was later also killed) and, with his radio man, Charles Kirkland of Kennett, Missouri, went to rally the confused and beleagured sector. Captain Spangler emphasized repeatedly that David must have known the risk he took in this action, and emphasized that, while all the officers except two staff non-com's were killed it was their timely action early in the conflict that saved the entire company from virtual anihilation. David was, apparently one of the last officers to be killed while the company commander was among the first. Captain Spangler conjectured that David might have been secure had he remained with his platoon; nevertheless, had it not been for his timely action the entire company (including his own platoon) would very likely have suffered much more extensive casualties. He added in passing that David's men simply worshipped him.

But there was one detail yet to come. The revelation started with a dream on May 20, 1973, the details of which I set forth in a letter to Douglas:

I saw David last night. He was sitting in a window

4

of a plain wall dressed in slacks and a plain white shirt. He appeared well, but his head was scarred. I was behind some type of transparent panel. Mother appeared, and went up to the wall to embrace him. I moved from behind the transparent panel to go closer, and every image disappeared. I moved back behind the screen and David and Mother reappeared, but then all quickly faded and I was awake.

This dream convinced me that David had also been wounded in the head. This conviction was strengthened by another dream on July 27, 1973, in which I saw David lying in the dirt—or mud—I could not be sure which. Only the right side of his face and right hand were showing. He looked quite brown in color. I became convinced that the wound on his head was on the side that was not revealed to me.

My convictions were confirmed on May 22, 1975, when Sergeant McKinney and his wife visited us at our home in Springer, New Mexico, and at the Vietnam Veterans Chapel. I asked him where David had been shot, and he informed me that bullets had literally laced his body. I then quietly said: "He was shot in the head too, wasn't he." The Sergeant looked up quickly with a startled expression on his face and nodded his head in affirmation as he said: "Yes, he was." At last we knew why David's remains had not been viewable.

Meanwhile, Douglas arrived home on June 2, and we learned that David's body would arrive in Albuquerque on the 6th of June. We made arrangements for his funeral on Monday, June 10, 1968, and journeyed to Albuquerque two days in advance. Here we met Lieutenant John Michael Pinkerton who had escorted David's remains. As we all approached David's closed, flag-covered casket for the first time, his mother collapsed on her knees before it, and in a wrenching, dry-eyed tone implored anyone who cared to answer: "What have I done to deserve this?"

The funeral director was immediately at hand with the ubiquitous smelling-salts and brought her, still dry-eyed to her feet. As it developed, it would have been far better for her had she been able to shed copious quantities of bitter tears. Douglas struggled for composure, but tears ran unwiped down his cheeks and fell upon the soft carpet like raindrops fitfully meandering down a leaf after a storm and finally dropping gently to the forest floor below. I was dry-eyed then, perhaps from the shock of seeing the variant reaction of my wife and son, but my turn would come.

During all this time, we were receiving cards and letters of condolence. Three of these are noteworthy. President Lyndon B. Johnson wrote the usual "Our hearts are made heavy" letter for next of kin.

Ironically, another Johnson—Louis E. Johnson, longtime friend and painting contractor when I had earlier been in the building business in Albuquerque—wrote eloquently with magnificent simplicity:

> Dear Friends:
>     May God be merciful and give you strength. We grieve with you.
>
>                     Mr. & Mrs. Louis Johnson

Mr. and Mrs. H.L. Anderson wrote equally expressively:

> Your dear David was our dear daughter Judy's first "love." We thought of him then as fine and special, and remembered him after they drifted apart always in a warm and special way.
>
> "Just as I am, though wilt receive
> Will welcome, pardon, cleanse, relieve
> Because Thy promise I believe
> O Lamb of God, I come—"
>
> We just know he is in heaven, at peace, and all his trials are over.

While I had been composed when first viewing David's casket, at the funeral—conducted by Chaplain William J. Cooper—I broke down completely. The funeral was especially poignant because David had written the words that were the central theme of his own funeral. I had shown David's essay: "The Prophet's and Their Times," to Chaplain Cooper who requested permission to use some of it in his remarks. He selected that portion in which David had commended the Greeks for their contribution to the material aspects of civilization, but paid an even greater tribute to the Hebrew prophets for their spiritual legacy. He concluded:

> After reading any treatise on government, say Plato's

6

Republic, and then comparing it with the Old Testament, one will see clearly that the Greek concerned himself with the mechanics of the things, while the Hebrew concerned himself with the spirit. A system is important, but only the living spirit of the ideal for which that system stands will capture men's imaginations and make that system work. The prophets provided the spirit that fuels our system today, and that is our debt to them. At the sight of the heavenly throne Ezekiel fell on his face, but the voice of God commanded: "Son of man, stand upon your feet, and I will speak with you." If we are to stand on our feet in the presence of God, what, then, is one man that he should debase the dignity of another?

Chaplain Cooper's rendition of David's words gave us a memory of dignity and beauty that will live with us always. True, life is for the living, but as we listened it seemed as though a measure of this expression would live forever.

We buried David in the National Cemetery at Santa Fe, and then continued on to our home at Val Verde. For most people this kind of traumatic experience is followed by going on in the old way and trying to live with the memory. For us, however, a skein of events had already been started that was to dramatically and irretrievably change our lives.

But first to the beginning of David's story.

## TWO

On January 3, 1940, President Franklin D. Roosevelt submitted to Congress a budget of $8.4 billion, which included $1.8 billion for national defense. David was born on the 30th day of that year. Four years later the budget would rise to $70 billion, with the President announcing: "This nation has become an active partner in the world's greatest war."

David?

Victor David Westphall III, first-born of Jeanne and Victor Westphall. His mother was born on July 15, 1915, at Highland, Wisconsin, and his father on October 13, 1913, near the tiny crossroads hamlet of Hebron in the same state.

February 10 was the last day for David and his mother at Mercy Hospital in Milwaukee, Wisconsin. He was born a robust 7 pounds, 4 ounces, and was more than holding his own. Before leaving the hospital with David, his mother had for her last meal a generous breakfast of apple juice, grapefruit, oatmeal, scrambled eggs with bacon, toast and coffee. Her roommate, Harriet Musolff, had the same although she and her newly born daughter were to remain for a few days longer.

At mid-morning of that cold, damp, cloudy day, a black Model "A" Ford coupe belonging to George Wickboldt pulled to the curb in front of the drab, brick three-story rooming house at 508 East Juneau Avenue. Formerly residences of the elite of the city, these dwellings had come down the economic ladder until they were the homes of persons who could afford only the meagerest of living facilities—like three dollars a week.

George was the special friend and weight-lifting companion of David's father. He had provided this modest transportation because the new parents had no car of their own. They lived at this address from September 15, 1938, when they were married to May of 1941. Juneau Avenue ran east and west, with 508 on the north side of the street. The buildings were separated by no more than a few feet.

The house was close to the sidewalk and one entered up a flight of some half dozen cement steps leading to the front door which opened upon a vestibule from which a stairway led to the upper stories. It was up these stairs that the Westphall family brought David to their room on the second floor.

As they ascended the stairs they were greeted by Charles Hollenbeck who occupied the room adjacent. Hollenbeck, a tall thin man of middle age labored at such odd jobs as he could find during these economically depressed years. David's father worked as a playground and social center director while studying for his B.S. degree, in Art Education which he received in June of 1939. He continued in this occupation from May to July 1941, when he assembled electrical controls for Cutler-Hammer Manufacturing Company. From July to October of that year he was the manager of the Wisconsin branch of the Chicago based Lien Chemical Company, specialists in cleaning and sanitizing toilets. From there he served as Program Director of the YMCA at Fort Dodge, Iowa, until he received a commission in the United States Navy on February 3, 1943.

The lodging occupied by the Westphall family was near the end of a hall where was located a bathroom for the use of the occupants of the four rooms on that floor. The new parents brought their son to a chamber scarcely 12 feet by 13 feet in size. The wall paper was of a garish design predominantly brown in color. The floor was covered with equally tawdry linoleum that had once been largely green in color. A few small throw rugs covered the most badly worn spots. A triangular shaped clothes closet in the southwest corner robbed area from the already meager dimensions of the room, while a corner window did the same to the northwest. Fighting for space between the closet and window was a nondescript brown day bed. In the corner along the wall from the closet was a table with a modest cabinet over it and a small stove beside it. Two kitchen chairs complemented the table, while a rocker occupied the remaining corner. Between this chair and the window, David's father had provided a new bright and cheery bassinet while the mother and son were in the hospital. This was the one blithe

9

accent in the entire room, and it was the focal point around which radiated the life of the newly increased Westphall family.

Water for cooking and washing came from the bathroom. While these accomodations seem spartan by modern standards, both parents were able to cope adequately because they were reared in homes of modest proportions. David's father, for example, had lived in his early youth on a Montana homestead where all water had to be carried seven miles from a pond shared by flocks of sheep. Drinking water had to be boiled and strained.

*   *   *

In 1967 David wrote in a brief autobiography: "In 1946 the family moved to Albuquerque, New Mexico. Because we couldn't afford to buy a house, my father decided he'd build one himself. Later he formed a partnership with another man just at a time when Albuquerque was the fastest growing city in the United States; the firm built thousands of houses, and my family went from what today would be called poverty to wealth."

*   *   *

In May of 1941 David and his parents moved to a seven room duplex at 2515 West Highland Boulevard furnished with 101 items of furniture loaned to them by Elizabeth Anhalt, his father's former speech teacher at Milwaukee State Teacher's College. The furniture had been in storage and Mrs. Anhalt thought to save the storage charges while concurrently aiding the family of one of her favorite students. But this relatively palatial living arrangement only lasted until October of that year when David's father accepted less pay in favor of more congenial employment and took a position as program director in the YMCA at Fort Dodge, Iowa.

Here the Westphall family increased to four with the birth of another son, Walter Douglas, on December 31, 1942. He was named after his father's middle name; however, like David, his family called him by his own middle name.

Scarcely more than a month after Douglas' birth, his father was commissioned as an Ensign in the United States Navy and moved his wife and sons back to Wisconsin where they lived for the duration of the war. They spent most of this time at the home of her parents at Viroqua, although they also lived part of the time with his folks at Hebron.

Ensign Westphall's first duty assignment was indoctrination training at Dartmouth College in Hanover, New Hampshire. During his stay there, with temperatures as low as -45 degrees, the mercury hit the lowest point in 85 years. The temperature in nearby Maine was -63 degrees.

David was now little more than three years old, but the attachment to his father was already profound. Some of the tricks they performed together were breathtaking for participants and spectators alike. Even before he could walk his daddy had held him overhead with both his feet in one parental hand while he shrieked with utterly fearless glee. Soon David's father learned to drop him from this position and catch him before he hit the floor. He had absolute confidence in his father, and his father in him. Some people thought it was horrible that they should take that chance, but they could have cared less.

Just a few days after his father departed by bus for the initial stage of his journey to Hanover, David awakened and insisted that his Daddy's bus was in the bed with him. From an early age David sometimes had strange notions that were difficult for his elders to understand. About this time his mother informed his father in a letter: "He likes to go down in the cellar. He goes way down to the coal bin and just stands there. I don't know what he thinks he is doing."

As the days lengthened into weeks with his father away, David was wont to stand by the window and state optimistically, but with just a tinge of a question: "Daddy will come back." Again, he would break in to routine conversations with such expressions as: "I want to give my Daddy a kiss and a bear hug." One day his mother took him uptown and he wanted to go every direction other than the one she was going. It developed that he thought they had gone to meet his daddy.

On March 7, 1943, Ensign Westphall was moved to Princeton University for two additional months of advanced indoctrination. David continued to miss his father. One day when he was uptown with his mother he started to scream. He had seen a bus and wanted to get on that bus and go to Chicago. His father had taken a bus there to meet a train on his way to indoctrination training. That night at the table he said: "My Daddy will get on the bus and my Daddy will drive the bus."

Late in March David's mother and father agreed that she would drive with the boys to Princeton. To do so she had to secure additional gas coupons from the local rationing board. They calculated the distance to be 1100 miles and gave her

11

19 coupons each good for 4 gallons of gasoline. By this time the family owned a small, four-cylinder Willys coupe. As it developed, this automobile was so thrifty with gas that it was able to make the trip with enough coupons left over for the ultimate return journey.

The journey was an arduous one for David's mother, with him and still ailing baby Douglas to look after on the way. But David was a perfect little gentleman and helped care for little brother as much as he could. While averaging about 300 miles a day, they completed the distance in four days, finding accomodations each night along the way.

The family would be together until Ensign Westphall left for foreign service. Meanwhile, he completed his instruction at Princeton and transferred to a highly technical underwater defense training at the Harbor Defense School on Fisher's Island, New York. He was there from early in May until the first part of September, and was then assigned to harbor defense duty at Rehobeth Beach, Delaware.

From December 18, 1943 to January 7, 1944, Ensign Westphall was granted leave before going oversees. He returned to Wisconsin with his family, and the leave was all too brief to visit the many friends and relatives on both sides of the family. This was war time will all its connotations of unknown perils in combat areas. A bravefront was the rule of those days, and was no exception in the Westphall family. Despite his most serious effort, David could not quite grasp that this would be a much longer separation then the previous one. Still, there was the anomaly that he seemed to understand it might be a permanent one.

When Ensign Westphall's leave was over, he departed for San Francisco and then, on January 28, for Guadalcanal in the South Pacific. When he reached this staging area he learned that there was a glut of harbor defense officers, and he was assigned to establishing fleet post offices and officer messenger mail centers in forward areas. He was to be in three invasions and spend two years within five degrees of the equator except for a month when he was hospitalized in Brisbane Australia, for a severe and persistent case of fungus infection. The highlight of his overseas career was developing the reputation for expediting mail more efficiently than anyone else in that entire war torn area.

For the next two years the war, along with the absence of his father, was to have a profound influence upon David's impressionable mind. Just a few days after his father left,

David returned from playing with some neighbor boys and stated that his name was on the draft board. He thought about this startling statement seriously for a few minutes, realizing that it didn't sound exactly right. Finally he concluded that the mother of his playmates had written his name on the black board.

He realized that his father had gone to San Francisco, but couldn't quite seem to grasp the immensity of his travels beyond that point. Whenever his mother took him to an area near the bus depot, he insisted that his daddy was "going to get off that old bus." One night he lay awake for a time. His mother asked him why and he replied that he was thinking of sending his cowboy gun to his daddy so he could put some tape on it. He remembered how his father had fixed it earlier, and assumed that he alone would be able to repair the toy because no one else had ever done anything like that for him.

But there was also an unusually close bond between mother and son. One night David held up both hands with all fingers outstretched and said endearingly: "If you had that many little boys they wouldn't be any trouble would they Mother?" She replied that they certainly wouldn't if they were as good as he and Dougie had been that day.

David had little games that he played with his mother. One of them occurred after he was washed and ready for bed. He would run into the bedroom and hide behind the open closet door. His mother would look successively under the beds, dresser, table, and chairs, and then on into the closet and ask: "Davy are you on the top shelf? You better jump down to Mommy or you will fall and get hurt." This was the signal for David to push the closet door closed on his mother and state triumphantly: "Here I am." His mother set forth the sequel to this pleasantry: "He undresses himself and puts on his pajamas, but can't button all the buttons. Then he sits at the foot of the bed and looks at a book while I get Dougie ready. Then very shortly we kiss each other good night, I pull down the shades, and the little darlings are soon fast asleep."

However, as the months stretched into years the yearning for his father never subsided. When the first photographs arrived from overseas he was so thrilled that he just screamed: "That's my Daddy." A little later he asked his mother if his father was coming home, to which she replied: "Not for a little while." He then voiced his oft repeated litany that he was going to get his Daddy off that old bus.

When anyone brought mail to the house, he would run to the door and hopefully ask: "Any mail for me?" One letter from his father had an account of how bulldozers pushed back the jungle growth. After that for a long time each night before he went to sleep he would say: "Goodnight Daddy in the jungle." His mother wrote: "He tries so hard to figure out just what it is like where you are, and mostly he wonders when that old bus will bring his precious Daddy home to us."

As time passed David talked so much about his father that Douglas would join in with such expressions as "Daddy write." Again, even at times when no adult conversation prompted the expression he would say: "Daddy come home." When shown his father's picture, he would say: "Daddy, Daddy." His mother wrote: "I really believe in his little maturing mind he can really remember his Daddy."

Almost daily David would ask when the war would be over so that his Daddy could come home. One night when his mother was kissing the boys good night he didn't want to kiss her. He said he was saving his kisses for his Daddy. She told him that they would all have lots of kisses for Father, and he replied that he would get some kisses from Dougie to give to him.

One day David brought home from kindergarten a paper on the care and importance of good eyesight. When his mother read it to him he mentioned several times that his eyes were good and that he could see far far away. Several nights later he said to his mother while she was washing her hair: "I can see far far away. I can even see my Daddy coming home." Just that simple thought seemed to make him very happy.

A few days later, when David was all dressed for school he turned the saddest little face up to his mother and said tenderly: "I wish my Daddy could come home." Then his mood turned defiant and he exclaimed with some vehemence: "I'm going to write a letter to those Japs."

Another evening at supper he announced a plan concerning which he had apparently given some thought. He reported that he was going to knock the "daily lights" out of the Japs. He had heard about knocking the daylights out of something, and turned that expression into a much cuter phrase.

Unlike many other youngsters, David seemed to be utterly naive about his cuteness and his mother wisely thought it

14

best to keep him that way. One day his grandfather made him sit on a chair and rest for a little. David gravely turned his face upward and sagely remarked: "Grandpa, you're breaking my heart." He couldn't seem to understand what he had said that caused smiles to be only half concealed.

One day David was grocery shopping with his mother and he remarked that he had seen his teacher. His mother asked if she had noticed him, and he replied: "Yes, and she smiled at me." That night his mother asked him who he loved and he said: "Daddy and Mommy and Dougie and Miss Huffer." It was well that he liked his teacher because that way he was good at school.

The ladies, particularly, thought David was cute. They would often ask him where he got his dimples. He didn't especially like to be fussed over; even at his young age he worked out a standard answer with which, no doubt, he sought to disarm them. He never ceased to be amazed at their merriment when he would quizzically reply: "At the dimple store."

David's mother early recognized his precociousness, as well as that of Douglas who was nearly three years younger. She wrote: "It is particularly unfortunate that the folks don't have any understanding of Davy's special nature." She also pointed out that Douglas paid more attention to some things than David did. She concluded: "They can both be great stuff, but in different ways and even this early in their lives one can detect signs of brilliance. Sometimes I just feel inadequate to bringing them up, but I will try to do my best."

David early showed signs of a phenomenal memory. When he was nearly six he recalled incidents of more than half his life behind him. In one instance his mother was washing him and he asked why Grandpa Westphall hadn't kept his farm. She informed David that it wasn't exactly his farm to keep, that it belonged to Old Grandma Westphall who lived in the big house. He answered: "Yes I know, she had the little kittens at her house and Grandma had the little house with the posts in the kitchen where I got my wagon stuck so Grandma took the wagon outside." David had been $2\frac{1}{2}$ years old at the time of this visit.

He asked so many questions that his mother sometimes requested him to desist for a time, that she didn't have the answer for everything. In general she tried to answer his inquiries as best she could, but very often one reply would simply lead to another question in endless progression.

Still, she recognized that his inquisitiveness was an admirable quality to possess.

At the end of 1944, David's mother enrolled him in the Junior Literary Guild. He enjoyed books so much that she thought the distinctive ones put out by the Guild would have a better influence on his impressionable mind than those of lesser quality. On March 8, 1945, David's mother wrote to his father:

> Davy's new Literary Guild book came today. It is "Wings for Per," a story about a little Norwegian boy who saw his country invaded and hid a radio in the mountains and printed the news and messages that England broadcast, and brought this news to his people. The Nazis almost caught him, but he got away on a fishing boat to England. He then went to Canada to train in the Royal Canadian Air Force and went back to bomb the Nazis the way they had bombed him. I must have read it six times to Davy. He and the book were inseparable the moment he got it. It is inspiring indeed. The pictures are lithographs cut from stone, printed in four colors. All the books he gets are beautifully illustrated, and for that reason alone I think they are all worth their price and some more.

*   *   *

When David's father was serving in the South Pacific during World War II, David's mother purchased for him a book titled WINGS FOR PER. This book was his favorite childhood possession. It could not then be known that he would one day serve his country in the war in Vietnam, and that his last official address and home would be Val Verde Ranch near Eagle Nest, New Mexico, in the foothills of Wheeler Peak, highest point in the State.

Prior to his departure for Vietnam, David designated a number of his books as a gift to the local school library. His last action before going to the bus on his way to Vietnam was to bring WINGS FOR PER to his mother and say: "I can't give this book, it's worth a million other books."

The conclusion of WINGS FOR PER reads: "Then I will fly up into the clear, washed air of spring and soar over the eagle's nest and over my home under the crag. Mother will stand in front of the house and clasp her hands in wonder. She will say: 'Look, Per has wings.'"

*         *         *

David was always popular with his peers and never lacked
for playmates. His best pre-school pal was Jimmy Christian-
son. One afternoon he accompanied Jimmy and his older brothers to the picture show. He enjoyed the company of the
other children immensely. When it came time for him to leave
them, it almost broke his heart. It seemed as though he wanted to stay with them forever. When it came time for him to
leave, he told his mother: "I love them so much."

But if the occasion demanded, he was equally content
playing by himself. A cellar window hole partially filled with
autumn leaves could be his foxhole from which he threw his
grenade with all the appropriate verbal accompaniments. A
visit to the park where he could climb among the rugged rocks
was always welcome. And when playtime was over, books
were always his special delight. He enjoyed having his
mother read to him endlessly. The Wynken, Blynken and Nod
book that he received when he was two fascinated him as much
as ever when he was aged four. One morning after his fourth
birthday his mother read to him from a new book of Bible stories. He then carried the book around with him for most of
the day and went to sleep with it under his pillow.

His mother, while not overprotective, made sure that he
did not roam the streets unattended. Still, he was filled with
more than the average amount of both mental and physical
energy for his age, and this characteristic landed him in oc-
casional mischief. One day he came home from Jimmy's all
smeared with roofing tar. They had taken the cover from a
pail of tar and played in it with sticks. Jimmy got a spank-
ing. While David didn't, the cleaning up process was probably a more grueling form of punishment. His mother had to
use kerosene on his hands, shoes and coveralls, then scrub
him with a manicure brush using lots of good hot water and
generous applications of soap. She then put clean clothes
on him, hid his shoes, and put on his night slippers so that
he couldn't go outdoors. Punishment enough?

One time David cut down some flowers, only a few, to
be sure, but they were his grandmother's favorites. His
timing was especially bad, because right at that time there
was a certain new toy gun that he wanted. To make the best
of a bad situation, he assumed the duty of disciplining himself. If he came down the stairs noisily, he would go back
up and come down quietly. He would also come back and

17

close the door quietly if he let it bang. And so it was with all the little things he could think of.

P.S. he got the gun. It was a plastic model of a .45 army pistol complete with belt, holster, and shoulder strap. He liked it better than any gun he ever had. Douglas also was privileged to select a toy. Naturally, for him, it was a truck—a fire truck with two ladders that could be put together and stood up on the truck. He took it to bed with him when he had his nap, and again when he went to bed that night. In the interim, he even let big brother Davy play with it some.

While David was unusually amiable with his playmates, he would fight back if pressed. One day two boys a little bigger than he was were both swinging at him. His mother was watching the affair and was ready to dash out if the play became too rough. He probably thought it was all in fun, but he was swinging back when suddenly his antagonists dashed away. As his mother reported: "David must have slugged them a little too hard for comfort."

David was utterly fearless of most everything, but he did develop one fear—that of dogs. Actually, this is a perfectly sensible fear where some dogs are concerned, but it came to be a phobia with him that extended to all dogs. It all started soon after his father left for overseas. A neighbor's dog, big furry Pete, habitually barked at everyone. He was getting old and quite deaf. The neighbor's children aggravated his behavior by pulling on his tail and fur. As a result of this teasing, he became surly and everyone warned not to go near Pete because he might bite you. David's mother wrote: "It seems almost tragic to me that this should have to happen to Davy when he isn't afraid of another thing in the world."

This fear of dogs came to a head when David started kindergarten. There were six or seven dogs in the immediate vicinity of the school. They would follow the children to school and then linger around for a time before returning home. One day soon after the start of school it was raining so the children were all inside. David spied a dog on the steps and didn't want to go in. When another little boy came along and walked right in without the dog moving, David decided to try it. His mother instructed him to just walk quietly up the steps and the dog wouldn't come leaping at him. When he reached the door without the dog moving, he opened it and shouted back to his mother: "I made it."

18

David was four months short of five years old when he started kindergarten on September 11, 1944. His first teacher was Helen Huffer. He was rather noncommital when he returned from his first day, but bit by bit it came out that they had a train and blocks to play with. Miss Huffer read them a story about Fuzzy Bunny, and the high point was that he had been both a giant and a cat in a play they had.

David had already enjoyed the benefit of vacation Bible school, so kindergarten was not an entirely new experience for him. Besides that, he had traveled extensively to locations where his father had been stationed before going overseas. His mother commented with a modicum of motherly pride: "He certainly does more talking and speaks plainer than any of the other children I have heard there. I wonder if his teacher notices these things. No doubt she will in a few days if she hasn't already noted them."

David was evidently quite a favorite with his teacher. One day he told her about his Gremlin book and she insisted that he bring it with him so she could read from it to the entire class. Another time she was particularly pleased when he drew a steamship and requested her to inscribe under it: "A little boat lived in a peaceful country and went out on the water every day."

David received satisfactory in every category of his report card for his entire kindergarten career. The comment at year's end regarding him read: "David is a lively little boy, enthusiastic over everything at school. He is popular with the group."

But the general implications of a circumstance on his very first day of school may have had a lasting and devastating effect on his psyche. He had a clip on his lip to secure a cut that he had sustained a few days earlier. The clip was removed the first day, but his lip had to be taped for several more days. His mother wrote: "It is too bad to have that tape on his mouth. He would be so much cuter without it."

A series of reports from David's mother to her husband in the South Pacific tells the story:

March 19, 1943—December 7, 1944

Davy had quite a tumble yesterday. We didn't see it, but we heard him land. He said he fell out of his hi-chair. His upper lip was bleeding a lot, but didn't

seem to hurt him too much. . . . This morning I let David
go to the park to play. . . . To make a long story short
he got hurt. He came home after he had been there about
half an hour. His face was scratched in two places and
both his upper and lower lips were cut. He said the airplane crashed. . . . The doctor disinfected the cuts and
put a clip on the upper lip. Davy was oh so good about
it all. The nurse said she never saw such a little boy
as brave as he was. The doctor put some gauze tape
over the clip and Davy said he had a mustache. . . .
Isn't it something the way all Davy's hurts are confined
to his face. Remember at Fisher's Island when he fell
out of bed and hit his tank, the only toy on the floor,
and cut his cheek—and then the tooth he knocked loose.
. . . There is about a square inch of skin off Davy's
under chin. I didn't notice it right away when he came
home so when I did I swabbed it with metephen. Davy
didn't like that very well, but just said it would help
grow some new skin. . . . Davy was hit in the nose with
a piece of ice at school today. . . . Miss Huffer. . . must
know by this time that he is always getting hurt in the
face. The skinned portion of his face that he acquired
last week hasn't healed yet and now he has a skinned
nose.

*      *      *

On October 14, 1960, David wrote:

Something's wrong with me and has been for years.
Maybe I'm more completely honest with myself than most
people. When I was in Los Angeles last week I went to
a library and finally found a book I've been looking for
on plastic surgery. Maybe I could have an accident to
my face and the Marine Corps would pay for repairing it
although it's a very messy process and takes a highly
skilled surgeon to do it right. I probably need a psychiatrist. This is the only thing that, really, ever has,
does, and ever will hurt me. Anything else whatsoever,
I feel confident to cope with, but after I look in a mirror
I am overwhelmed with a feeling of being lost, although
I'm not actually ugly. There's no way plastic surgery
can make me handsome, but it could make me better
looking.

*      *      *

On January 19, 1945, David's Grandmother Westphall died at her home in Hebron. His mother traveled from Viroqua to attend the funeral. When she returned he was not quite five years old. She mentioned to him and to her parents that Grandma had passed away in the little bedroom off the kitchen. There was no further discussion of the matter until the following May when she returned to Hebron accompanied by David. Almost immediately as soon as they arrived David closed the door to this bedroom. He didn't say anything, and his mother had no idea why he closed the door. Later some other children were running from room to room: David again closed the door. One of his cousins wanted the door open, then David quietly but firmly said: "No, this door has to be closed, there are ghosts in there."

David's mother was speechless, and his aunt sent the children outdoors to play. All of the elders in that household were silent for some time, for they had been in the presence of something they did not understand. They had already seen other examples of how David was about things like that. No private thoughts were aired. Perhaps some thought that his mother had talked to him endlessly about Grandma Westphall's death, but she had not. She was just as astonished by David's remark as any of the rest who heard. Her only discussion about ghosts had been that there weren't any. She wrote her husband: "He really isn't afraid of anything, but just talks and thinks way above our heads."

A few days later David and a friend named Johnny were playing in the cemetery. He later told his mother that he had sat on one of the little stones and said a prayer to a bigger one.

A month later David discovered a dead robin under a bush on the front lawn. His mother later noticed the robin and buried it in the garden. When David saw that it was gone he asked her where it was. She informed him that she had buried it. Right away he wanted to know if she had put it in a box. When she replied that she hadn't he thought for a moment then said he was going to place a stone to mark where the robin was buried. This he did, and as he reverently laid the marker down his mother asked him to say a prayer. He knelt and said: "Please God, take the baby robin's soul up near you."

21

# THREE

When David's father left Manila by ship for the United
States on October 25, 1945, neither he nor his family had
any idea that they would all soon move to New Mexico.
David was now approaching his sixth birthday and his
mother had enrolled him for a second year of kindergarten.
Douglas was nearly three, only a year younger than David
had been when their father departed for overseas duty.

Ensign Westphall was now Lieutenant Westphall.  He
was reunited with his family in Wisconsin on November 20,
after nearly 23 months of duty in the South Pacific.  The re-
union was joyous, of course, but in the background was the
nagging worry of a proper adjustment to post-war conditions.

He was released to inactive duty on February 5, 1946,
after two days more than three years of active service. Graduate school now beckoned.  The choice was the University
of New Mexico at Albuquerque where the climate would benefit his wife's chronic asthmatic condition.

Using some of his savings, they purchased a well-eq-
uiped and thoughtfully designed cabin trailer with inside
dimensions of 22' - 8" long and 7' - 10" wide.  While this
was a modest accomodation for a family of four, it was
downright luxurious compared to the one sparse room that
it had started out with when David was born.  The Westphall's lived in it for a few days before starting out on their
new adventure and found it to be crowded but comfortable.
For David and Douglas the trip promised to be the most ex-
citing experience that they had yet encountered in their
young lives.  Little did any of them realize the trials they
would encounter.

David's father kept a diary:

22

February 17 to 27, 1946. We left Milwaukee at
noon. . . the starter wouldn't work so we bought a new
battery, but it did no good. . . . had the brakes adjusted. . . traveled to Springfield, Illinois. . . . Springfield,
Missouri. . . . a sailor tried to pass us on a hill. . .
pulled over too soon and collided broadside with our
car. . . . Our little car was doing fine on the Ozark hills.
Everyone wonders how it does it. A twenty-five foot,
5000 pound trailer looks awfully large behind a Willys
coupe. . . . blowout on the right hand trailer tire at
Joplin, Missouri. . . . had a flat tire where the fender
had scraped it when the sailor ran into us. . . . slept
alongside the road at intervals that night (Jeannie says
who slept?). . . . new tire on right hand side of the trailer
was going flat. . . . slept for a time at Tulsa, Oklahoma. . . . arrived at Clinton, Oklahoma. . . . blew out
right hand trailer tire. . . . had a liner put in an old
4 ply retread. . . about three miles and that tire blew
out. . . . broke an axle trying to get the trailer off the
highway. . . . farmer was plowing and he pulled us off
the highway. . . put our lantern out on the highway and
went to bed. . . . had a reliner put in our one good six
ply tire. . . Amarillo, Texas. . . . flat on the left hand
trailer tire. . . . Wildorado, Texas. . . slept until
dusk. . . . reaching high altitudes and were stuck on
a couple of hills and had to be helped up. . . . Santa
Rosa, New Mexico. . . stuck on Santa Rosa hill about
four miles out. . . . fuel pump was not putting out for
such high altitudes. . . . to Albuquerque for parts. . .
lantern out on highway and slept there for the night. . . .
been warned of Palmo hill. . . had a fellow help us
over this hill so don't know if we could have made it
or not. . . . one more flat near Clines Corners and then
drove on to Moriarty. . . . they built up the fuel pump
eccentric arm. . . . warned of one more bad hill. . .
thought that it might snow. . . stopped for the night 26
miles from Albuquerque. . . . left the trailer behind and
went on into Albuquerque to look it over. . . . trailer
parks. . . bursting at the seams. . . . wasn't any room. . .
for our trailer. . . . bought a lot and then went back for
our trailer. . . . truck helped us to the Hilltop Cafe—
elevation 7300 feet. . . . dropped 2100 feet into Albuquerque. . . . arrived just at dusk. . . . decided it would
be a good investment to build a house on our lot and

went to bed. Postlude: We like Albuquerque very much.
New Mexico ably lives up to its slogan of "The Land of
Enchantment." P.S. We are going to build that house.
I have started my classes at the university. I am taking a
graduate major in history and a divided minor in English,
Art education and Philosophy. This all leads up to a
Ph. D. in American Civilization.

In Albuquerque David was disappointed to learn he could
not start school at mid-term even though he was six years
old. Meanwhile, David's father was hired by the University
as a student teaching assistant in addition to his own full
time studies. This paid $75 a month which augmented his
G.I. benefit of $125 a month. With no rent to pay because
of their mobile home located on their newly purchased lot,
they were able to manage.
Unfortunately, however, this lot was located on North
Glendale Street, west of the Rio Grande, several miles from
the University. For the sake of convenience, the Westphall's
purchased another lot at 1133 North Girard reasonably close to
the University and a grade school for David. David's father,
with the aid of his family, somehow found time to build a
garage on the lot. When this was completed in May 1946,
the family sold their mobile home and lot on Glendale and
moved into the garage. By September they completed the
house to go with the garage and moved into it, and David
started frist grade at nearby Monte Vista School. During
this time his father had continued as a graduate assistant
while attending summer school.
That fall the elder Westphall continued his own education and was hired as a teaching assistant with a pay increase
to $100 a month. But he still found time to build a larger
house nearby at 1145 North Princeton which was completed
for occupancy by the family in August 1947. They sold the
older house at a profit, as was now their practice, thus increasing their working capital. David continued his education at Monte Vista school.
Meanwhile, in October 1946, David's mother also became employed as the cashier at the Sandia Base post exchange at a wage of 50¢ an hour. She continued there until
May of 1947 when she was hired as the main kitchen super-
visor at Presbyterian Hospital. Her wage remained the same,
and she continued there until May 1949, when her time became more valuable at home.

With both parents either working or going to school, careful scheduling was required to care for the boys. They themselves helped a great deal by becoming self-reliant and trustworthy at an early age. From February 1947 to June 1947 their father assisted Roy Johnson in coaching track in addition to his classes. He received his M.A. degree that June. David was in school of course, but Douglas was frequently at home alone. During the summer sessions it was a common sight to see both sons playing on the campus lawn while their father attended classes. Their reliability was widely noted.

All this while home building continued in a modest way, interrupted from February 1948 to June 1948 when the father taught history at Albuquerque High school. He then went into homebuilding full time while concurrently working for his Ph. D.

In October 1949 he formed a building partnership with Clyde Davis under the firm name of Westphall & Davis. Each contributed $5,000 for a total initial capitalization of $10,000. The firm was dissolved in June of 1957 after having built some 3,000 houses. The Westphall's moved from time to time until they built a home in the Juan Tabo area of the Sandia Mountains into which they moved in August 1952. Later they built another home at Juan Tabo in which they continued to reside.

With the dissolution of the Westphall & Davis partnership, the Westphall's continued in the home building business under the name of Westphall Homes until early November 1966, when they sold all of their property in the Albuquerque area and moved to Val Verde Ranch near Eagle Nest, New Mexico. Meanwhile, the senior Westphall was awarded a Ph. D. degree in June 1956.

The frequent moves during the early years meant that David and Douglas were compelled to attend several different grade schools; however, their educational life was stabilized with their move to Juan Tabo. Here they enjoyed other advantages, as well. The family owned 80 acres of land; moreover, the western face of the Sandia Mountains was literally their back yard. Much of their roaming and exploring was done on foot, although they put their horses Cimarron and Gypsy to much more than average use. The parade grounds of a former CCC camp became their running track. Their home included an enclosed swimming pool and a spacious weightlifting area in the garage. More important perhaps, their father took time from his busy schedule to actively participate in these various activities with them, while their mother provided them with a wholesome diet and congenial home.

Here was an atmosphere conducive to the making of young athletes and they made the most of it; nevertheless, their formal education was paramount and they were also excellent students.

Whereas David had received a "satisfactory" rating in all categories of his report cards in kindergarten, during his first two years in Albuquerque he consistently needed improving in the categories of "Works and plays well with others," and "Obeys promptly and courteously." A comment by his second grade teacher, Laverne Schatz, was typical: "David often gets into trouble with other children in the room and on the playground. I have talked to him a number of times and I think he is really trying harder to be thoughtful and considerate. David could do much better work if he made good use of his time."

David's father answered this comment: "David's thoughtlessness isn't malicious. He simply has a good many thoughts of his own and at times they encroach unduly on the interests of those about him. As you say, I am sure he is trying to improve in this regard. We will be interested in your continued observation and comments."

By the end of second grade David had made progress although there was room for further improvement. Miss Schatz noted:

> David has improved throughout the year in his ability to get along with other children. At times he still shows a lack of emotional control, but I hope he can gradually overcome it.
>
> David has made excellent progress in his work. His growth in reading is especially commendable. He makes interesting and imaginative stories. He has done well in spelling. David has shown interest and ability in art work and in sports.

By the time David was in fourth grade, he was back to "S" or "S+" in all categories on his report card. At the beginning of the year his teacher, Miss McDermott, commented:

> David is doing fine work in all his studies.
> He definitely has "literary" and "artistic" leanings.

26

I do feel these could be and should be encouraged. His imagination is very acute.

David is quite a "sport"—he loves fun and play.

His father answered:

"Your observations are pleasing to us. We will encourage David in the fields which you emphasize."

At the end of the Year Miss McDermott wrote:

I have enjoyed working with David this past year. He is a challenging student and has great possibilities.

We have had our days of "misbehaving," but my corrections were only for this little fellow's good. A very pleasant summer to you all.

By the time he was in fifth grade, David had established himself as a solid student and cooperative member of society with only one chink in his scholastic armor—he found difficulty in mastering mathematics. His teacher, Dorothy Jamieson, noted this weakness, but commented in general:

David's enthusiasm, cooperation, and industry have made him an outstanding student. He works hard and has made many contributions to the class. He has shown satisfactory growth socially as well as scholastically.

His mother answered: "We are happy to note that David is doing so well in school."

To all intents and purposes David was now a happy well adjusted youth who fulfilled well his role in society. Photographs taken at this time show him smiling, trusting, and outgoing. As he progressed through high school, though, his photos often showed him more somber with a tinge of wariness as though to indicate that he was on guard against circumstances hurtful to him. While surely not even he knew all the reasons, they certainly centered around his athletic career. In this regard his father, in his enthusiasm for excellence for his sons in all regards, may have actually done him a disservice. This anomaly came about gradually and had its genesis when David first took part in organized athletics in Junior High School.

27

## FOUR

In September 1952, as a 12 year old 7th grader David
participated in his first organized athletics—representing
Monroe Junior High School as a halfback on the flag football
team. Tackle football did not start until the 9th grade. He
repeated the following year, and also participated in track
both years.

But in between seasons, on December 5, 1953, he won
athletic laurels of another kind. While still aged 13 and
weighing 120 pounds, he entered the novice weight-lifting
championships sponsored by the Albuquerque YMCA. He
not only won the 123 pound weight class, but also the special trophy as the best lifter for bodyweight in the meet.
His lifts were 165 pound clean and jerk, 115 pound two hand
snatch, and 105 pound two hand press for a total of 385
pounds. Considering that he was in competition with grown
men, his performance was considered phenomenal by experts
in the field. Even more sensational was his performance a
year later when he weighd 130 pounds and set a new 132
pound class state of New Mexico clean and jerk record of
185 pounds. To lift this weight of 55 pounds more than his
own bodyweight overhead at so young an age created quite
a stir in city's athletic circles.

The next spring, as a 14-year old 8th grader he ran 100
yards in 10.8 seconds. The following spring while in the
9th grade, competing in the city Junior High School track
championships he won the 50-yard dash 5.7 seconds, an-
chored his 440 yard relay team to first place in 44.6 seconds,
and was untimed in winning the 220 yard dash. Each con-
testant was permitted to enter only three events. The winning time for 100-yard dash was 10.8 seconds, David's time

of a year earlier.

But it was in 9th grade football with the Monroe Mustangs that David really began to show his athletic talent. There were six junior high schools in Albuquerque, so there were five games for each team. David's statistics in several categories of the games played tell how completely he dominated the play of his team. He gained 429 yards in 49 carries from scrimmage (8.75 yards average), completed 6 of 17 passes for 175 yards, caught 3 of 5 passes for 86 yards, intercepted 2 passes for 73 yards, returned 1 punt for 15 yards, as well as 2 kick-offs for 48 yards. In the 76 times he handled the ball, he gained 826 yards for 10.9 yards per effort. This was 30 percent better than the second best in this category on the team. At the end of the season Monroe was second in the league, and David was unanimously selected for the all-city junior high school team.

It happened that the football coach, Ollie Pembroke, had no assistance when David entered junior high and his father offered to help him. Ollie accepted, and this was the beginning of a long friendship between them. During David's 9th grade Bill Gentry was his football coach. David's father again offered his help, and it was accepted by Coach Gentry.

During these years David's father was in the building business in a partnership with Clyde Davis, and a plumbing contractor named Ed Curran had come into the association in a business way. During the summers of these years Hugh Hackett, coach of the Highland High School football and track teams, worked for the building firm. He didn't know that Davis and Curran, for reasons never made clear, opposed hiring him, but Westphall persisted because Hackett worked conscientiously and well. Moreover, they had become acquainted at the University of New Mexico where they were students. They found that they had been raised in neighboring towns in Wisconsin less than a dozen miles apart, but had never known each other there. They were interested in sports, and occasionally competed informally against each other in 50-yard dashes in which they were evenly matched.

During the summer of 1955 Coach Hackett again started to work for the firm of Westphall and Davis. Soon thereafter, however, he came to Westphall and explained that he would have to leave because of an ailment that impaired his work.

A little later word came back to Westphall claiming that

Coach Hackett had said: "No father is going to coach his son on any football team that I coach." This remark, if true, was in obvious reference to David's father having helped coach the junior high school team of which David was a member. The statement, again if true, did not present a valid comparison because the circumstances were entirely different. At Monroe Junior High there had been one coach with no assistants. At Highland High, where David was scheduled to start that fall, there was an ample staff of coaches.

David did attend Highland High that fall, but sustained a severe hamstring pull just a few days into the conditioning phase of the football practice. The coaches advised him to try and "run it out." This he tried valiantly to do, but it was obvious that this was no routine injury that would respond to such heroic treatment. Finally, David's father took him to see Ed Pillings, the trainer for the University of New Mexico athletic teams. Mr. Pillings correctly diagnosed that the injury was of a severity, nature, and location that only complete rest for an extended period of time would effect a cure. This was a crushing blow for David, but he took it with as good grace as one might under the circumstances.

The injury was so severe that David was hampered by it during the entire school year. He tried to run in track the next spring (1956), but was still bothered so resigned himself to running easily just to strengthen the leg. Both he and his coach feared that the all out strain of sprinting might only worsen the condition and set him back even further.

By the autumn of 1957 the injury had completely healed and David had trained himself into first-class physical condition. He was sixteen years old, not quite 5'-10" tall, and a muscular 165 pounds in bodyweight. His father had worked with him for the entire summer and he was ready for football in the fall. He knew that his lack of experience the past year would weigh against him, but he was confident of his ability and serene in his mental attitude toward the approaching season.

A portent of things to come occurred in the early season conditioning drills. Tommy McDonald, a former player at Highland High and then an All-American halfback at Oklahoma University, helped coach these drills until he had to report to his own team. He had also done so the previous year and was wont to run windsprints with the high school players, always winning easily. That fall with David running he did not do so. It was apparent to all that David was fast—very fast—at 40 yards or so. Some spectators conjectured that Tommy did not run against him for fear he might not win easily if at all.

Strangely enough, soon thereafter Coach Hackett announced that he was going to use David at tackle for the season. The reason the coach advanced for using David at tackle was that he had a lot of light, fast backs. Had the backs and linemen been permitted to run windsprints together as in previous years it would have been apparent that he had one light tackle who was considerably faster. Since David was also a little heavier and much stronger than the players in the backfield, one might reasonably expect that he would be an even better back.

David was entirely inexperienced as a tackle, but attacked his new position with total dedication. At a listed weight of 161 pounds, he was badly outweighed by other tackle candidates—as the season eventually shook down the two starting tackles weighed 215 and 236 pounds respectively. Even so, by sheer athletic ability David made himself (according to the coach) into the best tackle on the team. He started at that position in the preseason jamboree in which Highland, Valley, and Albuquerque High each played one period against each other.

When Highland broke from the huddle for the first play from scrimmage, an audible titter rippled through the crowd of spectators. David broke and ran to the line of scrimmage with such speed and enthusiasm that he was already set up there with the rest of the linemen still having almost half the distance to go. This was an incongruity that probably none of the assembled fans had ever seen before. David was entirely unaware of the stir that he created; he was simply starting and running at what was for him a normal pace. As a matter of fact, the one weakness that he displayed in his play during the game was that he sometimes penetrated across the line of scrimmage too rapidly and placed himself out of position for effectiveness. This was, of course, also a symptom of inexperience.

After the jamboree, a number of persons urged David's father to immediately transfer him to another school; in fact Jack Rushing, the coach of Albuquerque High, visited David's father about the matter. Coach Rushing was obviously agitated and tried to make it very clear that he was not there to advocate that David transfer, but that if he were to do so he would be welcomed with enthusiasm on his team. He also left no doubt that he considered David to be a far more valuable addition to any team as a halfback than as a tackle.

All of this appeared to be a clear indication that something was amiss at Highland High as far as David and football were concerned, but the Westphall family was reluctant to stir up what might be considered by some as a case of sour grapes by so drastic an action. Instead, David's father called on Coach F. M. (Tony) Wilson, city athletic coordinator. Coach Wilson was aware of the purpose of the visit before a word was uttered, but could offer no reason why David had been placed at tackle. At first he was reluctant to even approach the coaching staff for fear David might not even be allowed to play at tackle.

David's father told Coach Wilson that his purpose in seeing him was to seek information, and that certainly he didn't want to do anything to jeopardize David's chances on the team, but that any facts in the matter would be sincerely appreciated. Coach Wilson was universally esteemed as a gentleman and a competent former coach of high school athletics. He took this matter seriously and decided to see Coach Hackett despite his earlier reluctance.

While Coach Wilson's visit was terminated without a satisfactory explanation, shortly thereafter David was transferred to the backfield. Despite his lack of practice in the intricacies of a split "T" formation, in the first three nights of practice after the change from tackle he carried the ball 30 times and made 14 touchdowns (about the same as the rest of the backs combined). He also completed the only pass that he threw for another touchdown. Then came the Clovis game and David did not start, nor did he play in the first quarter. He carried the ball for the first time near the end of the first half and ran for a touchdown. This was the first time he carried the ball in his high school career. His father in the stands nearly went berserk when his faith in his son was so staunchly vindicated. In the second half David carried the ball six more times and made another touchdown. For the seven carries he made 58 yards, or an average of 8.3 yards per carry.

In the week of practice following the Clovis game he carried the ball only a few times although his late start in the backfield would have seemed reason enough for him to have received at least some practice in that skill. The only implied reason given by the coaches for this action was that they wanted him to perfect his "faking" into the line.

The next game was scheduled with Austin High of El Paso, Texas. Word of David's performance at Clovis was out and the El Paso Herald-Post reported: "Main Highland speed demon is Dave Westphall (No. 35) who is reportedly faster and shiftier than anything the Panthers have faced this year—and the Cats have faced some whizzes."

In the Austin game he was the leading ground gainer and maintained the 8 yards per carry average of his game at Clovis. But in the first quarter of the Austin game David further injured a leg that was first hurt in the pre-season jamboree. He played and practiced uncomplainingly with the bruise before the Austin game. On the strength of his performance in that game, he felt it safe to mention the bruise to Coach Hackett. The latter said there was a shin guard in the equipment room that would protect the bruise in practice. David came home elated. He told his parents that he might have avoided all the pain and misery had he spoken up sooner. The next night Coach Hackett gave him a narrow shin guard that did not cover the bruise because it was on the side of his calf.

That very night in practice David's leg was stepped on precisely at the location of the bruise and for months afterward the circle of the cleat marks was hard and lumpy with a soft spot in the center. One of David's teammates noticed the swelling and asked him if it was a muscle. David said no, that it was a bruise, and the other player replied: "You are so fast I thought it might be some muscle."

He did not start the Carlsbad game, although he had told the trainer he was sure his leg would stand up. He played much of the first half on defense and as a blocker; however, he was not allowed to carry the ball. David later told his father that he did not believe Carlsbad was as tough as either Clovis or Austin, and was confident that he could have run better against them than he had in the first two games. David played no more for the rest of the game. Highland was soundly trounced 28 to 7.

David's parents treated the leg intensively over the weekend and by Monday it was much improved, but Coach Hackett completely ignored David during practice. Finally toward the end of the week, David approached the coach saying that his leg was a great deal better and asked if he might get into the practice. His request was denied. Soon thereafter David impetuously went up to a halfback on offensive scrimmage and shoved him aside. The player asked: "Are you sure Hackett wants you in here?" David replied: "Yes," and proceeded to practice with abandon. The coaching staff was evidently so startled by this insubordination that it failed to either reprimand him or remove him from the scrimmage.

But there was apparent retaliation later. The next game was with Valley which Highland won 20 to 7. David was not allowed to play until the last few minutes of the game. He carried the ball four times for 21 yards and two strategic first downs almost to the goal line. Despite the boo's from the crowd, Coach Hackett then removed him from the game. The people assembled there seemed to think that this move was designed to eliminate any possibility of David making the subsequent touchdown.

On Wednesday before the Roswell game two of the halfbacks did not show up for practice (this would have been an unthinkable procedure for David) and another was injured. As David later said, they were near the bottom of the halfback barrel and he got into the practice. In five carries he made three touchdowns and 8 and 10 yards respectively on the other two. His playing was flawless.

The papers announced David as a probable starter for the Roswell game. The P-A System announced him as being in the starting lineup for the game. But he played not a single moment. Such a studied insult before 6,000 people was certainly at least in bad taste.

Coach Hackett now told David that he had not used him because he was afraid David might fumble. He said that David did not hold his hands in precisely the right "pocket" for hand-offs. What he didn't tell him was something that had been explained early in the season before David was at halfback. It seems that the coaching staff wanted this precise mode of holding the hands to facilitate faking by the quarterback. David had never fumbled in a game, and only in practice in hand-off drills when he tried to concentrate on the precise method of receiving the hand-off advocated by the coaching staff. It seems that there had been hours devoted to this special technique in the early season when David had not been practicing as a back. It would have been more reasonable had Coach Hackett paraphrased President Lincoln's statement that he would gladly hold General Grant's horse if he produced him victories, and said that

David could carry the football between his ears if he produced toughdowns.

At other times Hackett said that something must be the matter with David's eyesight because he "squinted" at the ball. Again, he stated that he was reluctant to use David in the backfield for fear he would reinjure the hamstring pull of the previous year. Oral tradition also had it that David was so adamant that he had to be threatened with expulsion form the team to make him hold his hands in the manner desired by the coaches. It was at this time also that there originated the vicious canard that David was clumsy with his hands and should, therefore, practice with a basketball. David patiently tried to take all of this obviously deliberate abuse in stride; the wonder is that he was as effective as he was considering the considerable strain on his psyche. He later staunchly denied that he had been anywhere near as intransigent as he was made out to be.

While David did not start the next game with St. Mary's, he did play and gained 54 yards on six carries. This was an average of nine yards for each time he carried the ball, and his total yardage led the Highland team. His over-all play was just as good. There was scant reason for keeping him out of the starting lineup, and he did start in the following game with Farmington.

He gained a team high 59 yards in 11 carries and had one touchdown in a loss to Farmington 14 to 19. But it was in other facets of this game that David excelled. On one occasion he dragged two would-be tacklers almost to the goal line. To their chagrin they learned that he didn't have the ball; instead, the fullback went unmolested to score. His faking was equally effective several other times. Seven times during the contest he blocked Farmington players completely off their feet. No other Highland back even approached this kind of blocking. He also completed one of the two passes he attempted. His only error of the game was on the other attempt. It was intercepted, but only a matter of inches would have meant a touchdown for Highland instead. The ball was intercepted more than 30 yards from where David threw it, yet he tackled the intercepting player after only a short gain. Thus it turned out to be just as good a maneuver as any of the several quick kicks on third down ordered from the bench. Highland was ahead 14 to 6 at the half. David carried the ball only once during the second half. Highland scored no more, while Farmington scored 13 points in the second half.

35

Perhaps the outstanding play of the game had been one kick-off return by Farmington where David covered his side of the field, then swung around to the other side and tackled the ball carrier from behind. Coach Hackett described it as the outstanding defensive play of the game, while the coach of the University of New Mexico football team stated that it looked as though every player on the field except David was going at half speed.

In the following game against Santa Fe, David was again demoted from the starting lineup. No reason was given to him personally or individually, but Coach Hackett criticized the faking of the Highland backs. Since he was the one who was benched, the approbation by inference would have to fall on him. In no other Highland game that year was a back tackled so many times by so many players as David was when he didn't have the ball. The blame more properly should have been acknowledged by the coaching staff. Assignments were fouled up and holes simply did not open. David was prompted to remark with a tinge of scorn: "If someone ever blocked a linebacker when I carried the ball I'd probably faint."

The next game was an elimination toward the state title and was a second contest with Farmington. David was returned to the starting lineup and played much of the game as a blocking back in a single wingback formation. Highland won 21 to 7 and then played their last regular game with Albuquerque High before going to the state championship game with Carlsbad the following week. As usual, David was the leading ground gainer against Albuquerque High with 130 yards and one touchdown in 14 carries. Highland won 28 to 12.

In the state championship game against Carlsbad the following week, Highland turned in a lackluster performance and lost 26 to 7. Despite his fine game against Albuquerque High the previous week, David did not start the game although he did play.

At the end of the season David was the only player from Highland to be selected on the all-state high school football team picked by the United Press. This was quite an accomplishment for a young man in his first year of high school competition who had started the season as a tackle, been switched to halfback the week before the regular season, who had been held out entirely from two games and had been used sparingly in others. And irony or ironies, he was selected to the second team as a tackle. Perhaps this was

the selectors' way of expressing distaste at the manner in
which David had been treated, for they surely knew that he
had played the entire season at halfback and had only practiced as a tackle before the scheduled games started.

It is usually accepted as common sense strategy to use
ball carriers the most who are the most effective as demonstrated by their average distance per carry. This rule was
completely ignored as far as David was concerned. He gained
489 yards in 71 carries for an average of 6.9 yards. The player with the second best average required 120 carries to gain
522 yards—a average of 4.4 yards per carry.

Meanwhile David continued to be an excellent student.
Early the following year he took the New Mexico Statewide
Test of Academic Aptitude which was distributed and graded
by the University of New Mexico. David made a 98 percen-
tile on this test. This meant that he had made a better score
than 97 per cent of the approximately 7000 students who took
it. The school administration was proud enough of this accomplishment to notify his parents with a glowing letter of
commendation.

That winter David lettered on the Highland wrestling
team that won the state championship. The wrestling coach
was Clem Charlton who later coached David's brother, Douglas, in football and wrestling at Sandia High School.

# FIVE

The following spring David was privileged to compete on
the Highland High School track team that was already a leg-
end. Coach Hugh Hackett and David got along splendidly in
track. This same Hugh Hackett who allegedly had stated
that David's father wasn't going to have anything to do with
coaching David in football at Highland high, publicly stated
on more than one occasion that he could teach David nothing
about starting in track—that his father had already coached
him to absolute perfection in that technique.

David immediately established himself as the top sprinter on this fabulous track team. Blessed with a phenomenal
start and explosive acceleration, his best distance was actually 40 or 50 yards—the traditional football player's test
for quickness. One night in practice Coach Hackett timed
him over 50 yards in what he insisted was under 5.3 seconds.
Two decades later, in 1978, the sensational Houston McTear
established a world's record for 50 yards of 5.25 seconds.
It is no wonder that Coach Hackett formulated plans for entering David in some indoor college meets at this shorter
distance, but they never matured.

This was, of course, David's first year of competition
and he had not yet developed the skills and power to hold
this blistering pace for even 100 yards. Even so he consistently ran 100 yards in 10 seconds flat and occasionally
9.9 (including a heat of the state track meet). Two years
later as a Freshman at the University of New Mexico, he
ran a 9.8 hundred in settling for second in a dual meet with
the University of Minnesota. Later that year he ran 9.7 in
placing 4th in the Skyline Conference Eastern Division track
meet. The winning time was a swift 9.5 seconds. He was
not quite as good at the 220 yard distance. His best high
school time for the longer distance was 21.9 seconds.

His normal sprinting stride was $7\frac{1}{2}$ feet long. One of his practice maneuvers was to run the length of a football field touching each 5 yard marker with the same foot for the entire distance.

David's other events were the 440 and 880 yard relays. Others on the team were Frank Gere, Jim Blair, and Tony Shaw. The order of running for the longer distance was usually Gere, Blair, Shaw, and Westphall. To take advantage of David's extraordinarily fast start, the order for the 440 yard relay was customarily Westphall, Gere, Blair and Shaw. This quartet was unbeatable throughout the season, culminating their efforts with new state records in both relays—43.2 for the 440 yard relay and 1:30.4 for the 880. The latter, however, was beaten the same day by Albuquerque High in 1:30.1.

The Albuquerque High triumph was due largely to Sammy Duncan, with whom David repeatedly vied throughout the season for top honors in the two dashes. There was never more than inches between them in the hundred (David always led by a comfortable margin at mid-race) although Sammy always managed to catch David at the tape. So it was at the state meet, although another black sprinter from Hobbs named Bradshaw Murphy entered the picture in the state meet. The order of finish in the hundred was Duncan, Murphy, and Westphall, with only inches separating the three. All were timed in 10 seconds flat. In the 220 Bradshaw beat Sammy, with David again third. The time was 21.8 in a preliminary heat. Normally both Duncan and Murphy outclassed David by at least a yard or so in the 220, but this time he hung in there with them so that the finish of all three was almost as close as in the hundred.

During the summer David continued to train rigorously: by fall he weighed a solid 175 pounds and was quicker than ever. He had experienced good relations with both Coach Hackett and his fellow athletes on the track team, and was cautiously optimistic that the discrimination against him in football of the previous season would not be repeated. He was wrong. This time, however, the cause seemed to be a clique of the players who influenced the selection of plays. Numerous ideas were mentioned concerning this possible conspiracy, most of them going back to the period in junior high school when David's father had helped coach the team he played on. One school of thought held that David was so much quicker than the other backs that the quarterback didn't call his play very often for fear he wouldn't get the hand-off to him on time. Also there appeared to be jealousy over David's athletic ability and scholastic aptitude. Then too, David was different than his peers. He wrote poetry, played musical instruments, enjoyed classical music, and didn't mind using a superior vocabulary.

\*          \*          \*

When David was five his mother wrote to his father who was overseas: "He really isn't afraid of anything, but just thinks and talks way above our heads."

\*          \*          \*

The season started with a 16 to 6 loss to Artesia in which David carried the ball 5 times for 34 yards. The next game was against Clovis and David had three carries for 30 yards and one touchdown. He scored again on a pass. Highland won the game 38 to 6. But the same discrimination against him as a ball carrier prevailed as it had the previous season. In these two games David gained 64 yards in 8 carries for an 8.0 yard average. The player with the second best average required 18 carries to gain 119 yards for a 6.2 yards average.

This was a situation that grated against David's sense of fair play. He did his share and more in every other department of the game. He wasn't asking for anything special, but he had repeatedly demonstrated that he was consistently good for two yards or so per carry more than any other player on the team. As long as he maintained this average, he felt that he should be used as a ball carrier at least as much as any other player. Common sense would indicate that he should be used even more than any other player, but he would have been well satisfied with even parity. Furthermore, he felt that it was robbing the team. Time after time that extra two yards would have meant critical first downs; furthermore, his point production would reasonably have increased. As it was, his average points scored per carry far exceeded that of any other player on the team. But he knew from experience that talking with the coaching staff would avail him nothing, and his father had learned the same.

And so it was that David talked to his parents about transferring to another school. He knew that he would be foregoing another season of the finest track coaching available anywhere. As a matter of fact he realized that he might

40

very well be passing up an opportunity to set a new state record in the 100-yard dash. After all, he had had only one year of experience. During that year Coach Hackett had expressed confidence that he would be able to do 9.7 the following year as a senior. The state record was 9.8 seconds. Hackett later expressed the same idea in a letter inviting David to come to the University of New Mexico on a track scholarship. As it was he transferred to Oklahoma Military Academy for his senior year which was a waste as far as track was concerned, but he did a 9.7 as a college Freshman the following year. It is entirely probable that he would have done the same as a senior on the Highland High track team.

David wasn't vindictive in transferring to another school. He just wanted out from a situation that was becoming increasingly intolerable to his sensitive nature. His decision was a traumatic one for him, and he made it on the basis of his high ideals—he just wasn't going to let petty people push him around.

Right about then another factor entered the process of making a decision. David's father had talked to Senator Clinton P. Anderson about an appointment for David to West Point. While no promise was given by the Senator, his attitude had been so cordial as to hold forth at least some promise. At the time, David's father was one of the leading home builders in the state as well as president of the Historical Society of New Mexico—both of which were of considerable interest to Senator Anderson. David and his parents felt that, if the appointment did come through, he would have a better chance of being accepted with a year of training at a military academy.

David's father made several telephone calls and learned that David would be accepted at Oklahoma Military Academy at Claremore; furthermore, that he would be more than welcome to try out for their football team even though the season had already started there. The family huddled over the matter, but the decision was David's to make. His mother and father promised him every cooperation, but would not attempt to influence him one way or another. He decided in favor of the transfer and immediately told Coach Hackett of his decision.

The coach was non-commital to David. Reportedly, however, he explained to his assembled team in a sarcastic tone of voice: "Well, our star player has quit." David really hadn't been a star, although he could and would have been had he been treated in merely a decent, humane manner. He had asked for no more, but thought he was entitled to no less.

On January 31, 1958, David was Senator Anderson's principal appointee to West Point. At the same time Thurston A. Griffith, Jr., was his principal appointee to Annapolis. Both were destined to lose their lives in Vietnam, Thurston being the first veteran from New Mexico to die in that war torn country. The photos of both would later be enshrined in the Vietnam Veterans Peace and Brotherhood Chapel. To this extent the Senator's benevolence had bound them to a common destiny.

When David arrived at Oklahoma Military Academy the football team had completed half of its 9-game schedule—all losses. The first game in which David played was against Sperry and OMA ended a 12 game losing streak with a 31-6 win. Reportedly the team looked completely new with David in the lineup. The next game was against Watts, this time a 40-12 victory. David scored on runs of 30 and 45 yards, and on a 85 yard kickoff return. The next game was against Holy Family of Tulsa. On the basis of games played earlier in the season these teams were rated even, but OMA won 34-12 while piling up 485 yards from scrimmage and 15 more from passing. The local newspaper reported:

## WESTPHALL LEADS OMA TO VICTORY OVER HOLY FAMILY

With David Westphall running wild, Oklahoma military Academy's high school football team won its third straight victory last night by turning back Holy Family of Tulsa 34 to 12.

Westphall, a speedy halfback from Albuquerque, N.M., scored three touchdowns, had another called back by a penalty, and broke loose for runs of 43, 41, 37, 33, and 22 yards during the game. A 21-yard run for his fourth touchdown was nullified by a penalty.

OMA closed out its season with a 21 to 13 win over a strong Cleveland team.

The team had employed a "T" formation, but when David arrived Coach Charles W. Brewer adapted some single wing plays to go with it in order to take advantage of David's singular athletic abilities. He played left end on defense and his quickness enabled him to be a constant thorn in the opposition's backfield in both passing and running situations. He was especially pleased with the surprisingly good downfield blocking of the team, which he had noted to be conspicuously lacking at Highland High.

Two factors accounted for his remarkable showing at OMA. Admittedly, the school did not play the caliber of teams as the school he had left in Albuquerque, but there was a more important factor. At Highland he had been playing under constant tension for fear he would do something which would earn him an unwarranted demotion or other censure. At OMA he played relaxed and was inspired to excel by his teammates. It was fairly common for players from the Junior College team to challenge him to score a touchdown in certain situations. In a surprising number of instances he rose to the challenge and did score the touchdown demanded. He was an instant hit with spectators at games who cheered for him lustily. For one example he had just broken a tackle in an especially forthright manner and a spectator shouted loudly from the stands: "Don't get in his way if you don't want to get hurt."

Before the Holy Family game David wrote:

A boy on the college team told me last night that when he was on pass to Tulsa he talked to the sports editor of the Tulsa Daily World and that that paper is sending a reporter to our next game. Also Tulsa U. is sending a scout.

For the short while that he was there, David created quite a stir in a limited sphere of Oklahoma football fandom. His particular friend was Hugh Key who lived at Norman. Hugh reported that he had heard glowing reports about David in the football circles of the University of Oklahoma there.

David did not participate in any extracurricular activities other than football because he spent all available time studying for West Point exams. He received the very finest of extra coaching from the faculty at OMA; however, as he reported: "Despite excellent instruction and outstanding scores in the physical and english portions of the test, I still couldn't make up lost ground in math and science and failed those portions."

Carleton R. Crowell, the head coach of track and field at West Point, was very much interested in having David attend there. He wrote to David's father offering every encouragement for David's attendance at the Military Academy.

But David also heard from Hugh Hackett who had become track coach at the University of New Mexico. Despite his differences with Coach Hackett in football at Highland High, David wrote him a letter of congratulations when he heard that Hackett had been appointed to the track position at UNM. Coach Hackett answered:

May 15, 1958

Thank you for your letter I received a couple of weeks ago. I hope you received your appointment to the academy this year but if you did not receive your appointment and need additional schooling I would be very happy to have you attend the University of New Mexico.

I hope to have a very fine team and our really great need is a fine sprinter. I am sure I could recommend you for a scholarship and I would consider it a privilege to work with you again in track. I know you could have run the 9.7 this year.

I will be at the University starting June 1 and would appreciate your dropping in to see me if you are interested.

Sincerely yours,

Hugh Hackett

David accepted the scholarship, but his father concurrently awarded another that more than offset the value of the one to David. This aid was given to a graduate student who had lettered in some sport at the University. The grant was arranged through Pete McDavid, the athletic director at UNM. By request of David's father, the donor remained annonymous.

## SIX

When Coach Hugh Hackett offered David a track scholarship to the University of New Mexico, David was confident of receiving the very best coaching available in that sport. But he was not nearly as optimistic about his football future in Albuquerque. He feared that the old animosities and jealousies might crop out in college as they had in high school. In the end he decided to accept Coach Hackett's offer. His experience in freshman football was reasonable, and that in track everything that he could expect. But he could not foresee the storm clouds of vituperation that would descend on him in football during spring training of his freshman year and the regular session of his sophmore year.

Freshman football was regarded by the coaching staff as a season for looking over new material and evaluating prospects for the future rather than a serious effort to win games. Newly appointed Freshman coach Don Chelf, former All-Big 10 tackle from the University of Iowa, inherited a squad that was rated as possibly the most talented and huskiest freshman team ever assembled at the University of New Mexico. The squad numbered 29 who were on scholarship and 40 more turned out for practice on their own. There were 12 states, including New Mexico, represented among the players.

When practice started David was on the first team. The night of practice after the first scrimmage he suffered amnesia from a blow on the head and missed two practice sessions. This was the first practice he had ever missed in his entire football career. When he returned he wasn't on any team. Finally he was put on the last team and ran Montana plays against the varsity. He handled the ball four times. On

one play he ran for a touchdown and on another passed for a
second touchdown. He picked up 12 yards on two other carries. The next practice he was again on the first team.

In the first game against the Arizona wildcats , David
did not start although he did play in a losing cause 33 to 0.

The next game was against New Mexico Military Insti-
tute, and David's team lost again, this time 31 to 0. David
started the game and was held to 13 yards on six carries, but
his line was very inept and tacklers were upon him almost
before he received the hand-offs.

Defensively he kept in mind the factors of proper angle of
pursuit, proper stance on tackling contact, and decisiveness
of action. He made three of the first half dozen tackles in
the game—one for a loss and the others for short yardage.
After that most of the plays were directed to the other side
and he covered nicely even there while still not over-commit-
ting himself. Only one of the five touchdowns made against
his team occurred while he was in the game.

Losing was now getting to be a habit for the University
of New Mexico freshmen, and they were again blanked in
their next game against Fort Lewis. David once more started
the game, and this time played most of it. He made more
tackles than the rest of the defensive halfbacks on his team
combined. Offensively he made 59 yards in seven carries.
The rest of the backs on his team gained 78 yards on 30
carries.

In the final game against the Denver University yearlings
David was named a game captain along with Charles Cum-
mings, a guard. David played his usual steady game on defense, and scored three of his team's five touchdowns. He
intercepted a pass for a 67 yard touchdown return, caught a
scoring pass also for 67 yards and plunged for another score
from the one. He made 66 yards on nine carries, while the
rest of the team used 24 carries to gain 101 yards. New Mexico added 270 yards on 14 out of 28 passes.

All in all this had been a productive season for David.
If, as was publicized, freshman football was calculated to
see what new players could do, he had ably demonstrated
his ability. Among other items, for the four games he had
led in total yards gained (141), average gain per carry (6.1),
scoring (18 points), average gain per pass reception (67),
total yards gained from pass receptions (67), and average
gain per pass interception. His blocking and defense against
running plays had also been excellent.

His team high average of 6.1 yards per carry from scrimmage was extraordinary considering that his team was badly outclassed in three of its four games.

Meanwhile, David wasn't resting on his athletic laurels alone. Carlos Salazar, in his "It Says Here. . . " column of the Albuquerque Journal for March 4, 1959, tells interestingly of his scholastic achievements as well:

> While on the subject of UNM athletics, it might be said that Hugh Hackett, Lobo cinder coach, is mighty happy these days. . . not because his athletes are progressing so well on the field, but because they've tapped gray matter in the classroom as well.
>
> Hackett, the builder of champions (seven times in a row) at Highland High, has a 30-man cinder crew that averaged B- in the first semester grades.
>
> Jim Ransom, one of the many former HHS trackmen now enrolled at UNM, leads the parade. Although only a frosh, Ransom has straight A's for 18 semester hours. He majors in English. Ransom is a sprinter on the track team.
>
> Another Frosh dashman, Dave Westphall (who also doubles as a halfback in spring football), is averaging 2.3—a B-plus in parlance that you and I can understand. Westphall majors in history.

That March, also, he was pledged by Sigma Alpha Epsilon fraternity. The president of that fraternity reported to David's parents: "We are very glad to have pledged your son this past Monday night. We know he is both a high-minded and courteous gentleman."

In December David competed in a series of indoor intersquad track meets. He had done 60 yards in 6.3 seconds in practice, but his best time was 6.4 in any of the meets. He did win all of the races. He also was on a winning 440 yard relay team that turned in a sizzling 42.3 seconds—probably the fastest 440 relay he ever participated in. The other members of the quartet were Bobby Collins, Ken White, and Dick Howard.

That spring he had to decide whether to continue uninterupted with track or participate in spring football practice. He chose the latter knowing full well it might hamper him in track because training for the two is not necessarily compatible.

David had participated in freshman football in the fall

of 1958 with only a minimum of the unpleasantness that had characterized his participation in that sport at Highland High School. Still, there were subtle rumblings indicating that an adverse tradition that had grown up about him as a football player had not been laid to rest. As a result, early in 1959, his father, with David's concurrence, hired a private investigative service to look into the matter of the earlier intrigue at Highland High. The purpose of the report was to secure some background for a determination as to whether or not David should continue at the University of New Mexico, or whether the adverse tradition would effect his football playing there.

The report on the investigation was released early in March while spring football training was in progress. It was very definite in its conclusion that a cabal of fellow players at Highland High had worked against David's interests there and that the coaching staff had been unwilling or unable to correct the obvious injustices. It also indicated that David's case was pretty much common knowledge in athletic circles in Albuquerque and that, generally speaking, one was either for or against David Westphall—there didn't seem to be much common ground. But it also seemed to hold forth some hope that the coaching staff at the University of New Mexico would not be influenced by the tradition.

As it turned out the "word" had undoubtedly gotten to the UNM football coaching staff. At Highland he had been rated as clumsy with his hands and was advised to practice with a basketball. In high school at the Oklahoma Military Academy he was considered a good ball handler and especially good as a pass receiver. He had also demonstrated this ability as a freshman at UNM. Now during spring football practice he was again considered clumsy with his hands and it was again suggested that he needed basketball practice. The fact is that he almost never fumbled the ball if the coaches would stay off his back—what more did they want?

*       *       *

> At the sight of the heavenly
> throne Ezekiel fell on his
> face, but the voice of God
> commanded, "Son of Man stand
> upon your feet and I will
> speak with you." If we are to

stand on our feet in the
presence of God, what, then,
is one man that he should
debase the dignity of another?

David Westphall

*         *         *

At Highland High he was considered inadequate on defense. This had not been the case at Oklahoma Military Academy; furthermore, he had demonstrated superior defensive ability as a college Freshman. Now his defensive ability was again suspect.

One spring football intersquad game was held at Roswell. At the half Marv Levy, the head football coach, came into the stands to talk to some high school coaches and other people from the southern part of the state. One of them said to Coach Levy immediately upon his arrival in their presence: "This Westphall boy is sure looking good on defense don't you think?" David had just come up from defensive halfback and tackled an opposing ball carrier for a substantial loss. Levy replied: "He's got a lot of spirit." This, of course, was not an answer to the question and his tone of voice was so noticeably lacking in enthusiasm that the matter was immediately dropped.

The coach did not notice the presence of David's father seated no more than five feet away. Soon thereafter he stood up and still was not perceived. Several times thereafter for the next few minutes he stared the coach straight in the eye and after an embarrassingly long time was finally recognized. His purpose was to avoid hearing possible further discussion about David without his presence being known.

It might be mentioned that David's support among the athletic fraternity had always been strongest outside of Albuquerque. One notable example was the fact that he had not even received an honorable mention on the all-city team while at Highland High during his junior year, yet was placed on the all-state team.

Following the Cherry-Silver game of February 28, 1959, David's father sent the following note to the Sports Editor of the Albuquerque Tribune:

In compiling your list of "stars" among the halfbacks

you might have considered their record against that of
David Westphall who gained 94 yards on five carries
(1 T.D.), caught a pass on a diving leap for some 20
yards more, made his share of tackles on defense,
covered faultlessly on pass defense, was a couple of
yards behind a teammate when the latter intercepted a
pass and ten yards downfield passed him to make a key
block that sprang him loose for a touchdown, and on
one play was the only player on the red team who wasn't
suckered by a quarterback keeper to the weak side and
made the tackle that averted a touchdown for the silver
team.

Another example of partiality and misleading reporting
occurred right after the completion of the third of the four
games. Carlos Salazar reported in the Albuquerque Tribune
of March 20, 1959, that a certain fullback (call him X) was
the leading ground gainer for the silver team at the time.
The fact is that, at the time, David had 162 yards in 13 carries for an average of 12.5 yards per carry. While player
X had carried the ball 24 times, he had been held to 144
yards—an average of 6.0 yards per carry. In the four spring
games the leading ground gainer required 40 carries to make
235 yards, while David gained 185 yards in only 16 carries.
After completion of the four games David knew what his
record for them had been because his father had kept meti-
culous statistics. He went to Coach Levy and courteously
brought up the subject of this data. Levy brusquely informed
him that he wasn't interested in statistics in spring football.
When David pressed him he said what he looked for was the
kind of attribute that could be summed up by the words desire
and hustle. A bit later he contradicted himself when he said
the main thing he scrutinized in spring football was play ex-
ecution.
Perhaps all of this should have been sufficient indication that David simply wasn't going to get a fair shake in
football in Albuquerque. The sentiment against him was
simply too deep-rooted. One malicious example occurred
after David left UNM. The coaches there took the bother
to inform those on the Marine Corps football team at San
Diego that they considered him weak on defense. When he
went to the Marines he was told in his first football inter-
view: "Westphall, you're weak on defense aren't you."
David replied: "No Sir." The interviewer than said: "Your

college coaches say you are." David replied with a tinge of irony: "If they say so it must be so." He left with the impression that they intended to find out for themselves.

All of this was an especially traumatic experience for David's father because he knew that his own interest in his son's football career was at least partially responsible for David's troubles. He could see what was being done to his son, but seemed powerless to help. In fact, there was at least some indication that he had tried to help too much and had only further intensified the notion that David was a problem case and needed to be disciplined. If only his tormentors could have seen that they were crucifying him instead of disciplining him.

Why did David return to the University of New Mexico for his sophomore year when he knew that the cards might be stacked against him? Perhaps the most significant reason was that he felt that he had already run away too much. He knew that this could be interpreted as an indication that he was simply hard to get along with, and might follow him wherever he went. And so he decided to stay.

When football practice started that fall David's father studiously remained away from all but a very few practice sessions. He thought that if his presence at practices were a detriment to David's relationship with a football career, even in some intangible way, he was perfectly willing to stay away.

As a matter of fact he attended only two practice sessions. The first was a Saturday night game-condition scrimmage. David played the entire game, and played well. Shortly thereafter he was demoted, evidently for poor ball handling. He had sustained a finger sprain. Other players sat out practices because of such minor ailments as tape rash. Because of the peculiar circumstances of David's football career in Albuquerque, he always felt if he missed any practice time at all it would be held against him; consequently, aside from two days during his freshman year that he was held out for observation for amnesia, he never missed a minute of game or practice time because of injury in his entire football career.

This doesn't mean that he had not been hurt. He was, after all, flesh and blood. But he played regardless. He had always had a high threshold to pain. Once when he was a baby his father rather clumsily pinned on a diaper and investigated to see what David was squirming about.

51

To his horror he learned that he had pinned the diaper to a fold of skin.

In the first game against New Mexico State University of Las Cruces, David was in the game for only one play. This was a kick-off return by NMSU's Pervis Atkins. David covered his own territory, then caught Atkins from behind. This was no mean defensive feat, because that year Atkins was rated as one of the fastest backs in the nation. No coach could reasonably ask for better defensive play.

David's father saw one more practice session after the UNM loss to NMSU. Three things stood out in his memory. Once a starting fullback fumbled the ball. One of the coaches shouted: "Fall on it. Fall on it right now!" The player walked over to the ball, picked it up, and threw it to the coach. Nothing more was said.

Another time David was playing on defense. The defensive formation amounted to virtually a nine man line with the defensive halfbacks relatively deep and wide. In spite of the strength of the line an offensive halfback maneuvered outside the end toward the side where David was defending at defensive halfback. The ball carrier had two man interference in front of him. During his career David repeatedly made more tackles for a loss coming up from halfback than any of his peers. This time, however, he was aware of the massed interference confronting him and realized that he was all alone until reinforcements could arrive. He elected to jockey the ball carrier and his interference toward the sideline until help came up.

His thinking was that if he crashed, the ball carrier might get clear away for a touchdown. David isolated the ball carrier to a narrow corridor along the sideline and the other defensive halfback was able to come over and make the tackle after about a seven yard gain. To give ground and avert a touchdown was the only reasonable strategy, yet David was immediately chewed out for not crashing and turning the play in. This defensive maneuver was clearly the responsibility of a defensive player other than the halfback. This kind of treatment prompted some of the other sophomore players to make the unsolicited comment that whatever David did seemed wrong.

Shortly thereafter three other backs were defending in a formation that had players all over the secondary. One of these was Don Perkins who later played fullback for the Dallas Cowboys. The same ball carrier again got around

52

the end—this time all alone. Perkins was sucked in completely out of the play. The other two defensive players each had a shot at him, but the ball carrier went all the way for a touchdown. Nothing at all was said by the coaches.

On Wednesday before the Colorado State game, backfield Coach Bill Weeks told David: "We have serious doubts as to your ability to hang on to the ball." David told his father: "They've got me thinking that maybe I am the clumsy oaf they try to make me out to be." As a result he felt that if he ever got into the game a single fumble would fix him but good. It so happened that without even the slightest indication that he was even going to play in the game, he was sent in for an obvious scoring situation. His entire attention was centered around not fumbling; nevertheless, he did fumble. The handoff was clean and David reached the line of scrimmage where he was met by a defender who missed the tackle but hooked David's ball carrying arm.

Even then David might well have fallen on the ball as it bounced away from him; however, he was so horrified at seeing what he honestly considered his one chance go glimmering that he froze into uncertainty and Colorado State recovered. It seemed as though his entire football career had come down to this single moment. He was benched and studiously ignored by the coaches for the rest of the game. Even after it was over, not one offered him the slightest word of encouragement or even chewed on him about the mistake as was their wont in David's case.

That summer he had attended a Marine Corps platoon leaders training program at Quantico, Virginia, where he earned the highest physical fitness score in the entire battalion and was on the honor squad of the honor company. He now turned to the Marine Corps for the solace that he found to be utterly lacking among his coaches at the University of New Mexico. One word of encouragement from them would have dissuaded him, but they were not willing to bend even that tiny bit.

*         *         *

In a letter of January 5, 1971, David's father wrote to his wife.

For what comfort it may bring, please share with me the knowledge (as communicated to me by Capt. Spangler that David's men simply worshipped him. He has been

53

through his agony with the callousness of his fellow men, and has found his place and his peace.

*      *      *

David's parents could not honestly argue against his decision to join the Marine Corps, or at least to remove himself from the environs of Albuquerque where he had met so much humiliation and pettiness. Had they known the results of the earlier mentioned private investigation before he enrolled as a freshman, they would certainly have counseled against him doing so, and he himself would no doubt have been loath to again enter that hostile environment. Both he and his parents were fully aware that his leaving under the circumstances that existed would be construed by many who were uninformed as to the facts as running away from an unpleasant situation. His year at Oklahoma Military Academy had been so pleasant by contrast that he simply could not see himself further pushed around by circumstances in Albuquerque over which he apparently had no control.

After David joined the Marines his father phrased a letter to head coach Marv Levy explaining David's entire football career in Albuquerque, but never sent it. By 1962, however, Backfield Coach Bill Weeks had become the head coach at UNM. Early in the season his players were being criticized in the press for not performing well at crucial times. David's father used this fact as a reason for writing a letter to Coach Weeks.

The letter partially concerned some UNM players who had been hired by Westphall Homes the past summer in the construction of an apartment complex. Westphall explained in part:

> Bolstering crew confidence as a primary technique is not a common practice in the building business; however, it is the only way I could have, in the brief time available, welded this group of inexperienced youngsters into a competent, professionally operating crew.

He then reviewed briefly David's football career at UNM culminating with Coach Weeks' statement to David: "Westphall, we have serious doubts as to your ability to hang on to the ball." Now he challenged Weeks to name an instance in a previous game where David had fumbled the ball. In

54

this way he pointed out that Weeks should have held himself accountable for David's fumble in the Colorado State game.
Coach Weeks replied:

> I received your letter of November 5 and appreciated your constructive suggestions as to building team confidence and morale.
> I am sorry that you do not feel your son David was coached properly during his short career here at the University of New Mexico. We felt him to be a very outstanding prospect and were quite disappointed when he elected to leave school and enter the Marine Corps.
> If you should ever care to discuss David's career here or our present handling of the Lobo team, I would be most happy to accomodate you.

David's father did not avail himself of Coach Weeks' invitation to discuss David's career at UNM in person. He thought nothing was to be gained by reopening old wounds.

Publicly, also, David never looked back. Whatever regrets he may have had he took with him to an early grave. There can be no question, though, that his love of football and the unkind cuts he suffered as a result were immovably instrumental in shaping his life—and death. He was an anomalous young man who went through his brief span of years never wanting to hurt anything or anyone even if it meant he himself being hurt instead. He was never really understood by his peers, and only a few bothered to try. To his elders he seemed aloof when he was really only shy. To his God he must have been one of those rare entities who live essentially in harmony with right, even though it be contrary to the norms established by man with his feeble grasp on the great significances of life and living.

# SEVEN

In David's effects, following his death in Vietnam, were five envelopes each bearing the words written in his characteristic handwriting: "David loves Lynne." He probably wrote these enigmatic words in December 1960, a month or two after he withdrew from the University of New Mexico and entered the Marine Corps. If he wrote them then there is no indication why, when he kept so little else, he saved these envelopes through his marriage to Lynne Willmarth and his subsequent divorce from her—indeed until the end of his life.

Mary Lynne Willmarth was born October 27, 1940, nine months after David's birth. They were classmates at Highland High School in Albuquerque. When they were sophomore's in 1956 she wrote on the first page of his yearbook:

David,
Best of luck to a wonderful friend.

She was the only girl to inscribe a message in David's yearbook that year, and one of a total of only five students who did so. There may have been so few because he was naturally shy; moreover, he was somewhat despondent and withdrawn at the time because he was compelled to sit out that entire year of athletics on account of a pulled hamstring. It is also about this time that he was visited with a fixation concerning the unpleasantness of his facial appearance. Collectively, he was an entirely attractive specimen of young manhood, but his nose was different than most. Instead of the usual indentation at the bridge, it slanted more or less directly down from his forehead. It was certainly not an unpleasing facial characteristic, but it was different than most

56

and unaccountably vexed him. Perhaps significantly, he would not allow a photo of himself in the school yearbook that year nor the next.

David and Lynne came to see more of each other during the latter part of their junior year at Highland High School and the following summer. In the fall of 1957 David transferred to Oklahoma Military Academy, and they corresponded while he was there. The following year they were freshmen at the University of New Mexico and they gradually became more inseparable through that school year and into the following one. Early in the fall of his sophomore year, for reasons set forth above, David decided to leave the university and join the Marine Corps.

That summer (1959) he had attended a platoon leaders training program at Quantico, Virginia, so the boot camp period of his new enlistment presented no substantial difficulties for him. Ironically, while he had been beset from every quarter in Albuquerque football circles as athletically too independent in his thinking—hence difficult to coach— he was immediately singled out at the San Diego Marine Corps Recruit Depot for the important job of platoon right guide. David reported: "I'm responsible for, and hold almost the power of life or death, over a platoon of seventy." He regretted mildly that this post was almost certain to preclude his participation in football that fall, but was heartened because it gave him a good chance of being top recruit in the depot.

During the time that he was at San Diego he had corresponded with Lynne, but had not mentioned her in any of his letters home. But this was soon to change. He spent much of his time with her while on leave and asked her to marry him, but did not tell his parents. He first informed them of his intention in his second letter to them after he returned to California for further training at Camp Pendleton. In this missive, dated April 17, he asked them to advance him $10 a month in addition to the sum that he was then borrowing from them to pay for land he had purchased in Brazil. He needed to buy Lynne an engagement ring.

He had feared that his family, especially his practical minded father, would be upset with the idea of his becoming married while only a private in the Marine Corps. He hastened to add that they would not be married for at least another year.

Concurrently David was concerned with making the San

Diego Marine Corps Recruiting Depot football team. He returned from leave following completion of his boot camp training in April 1960, and learned that spring football practice would start on May 9. This practice was essentially for the coaches to look over new material since the proven veterans of the team weren't even practicing. David was on the first team in these drills and was one of two halfbacks retained for regular practice which was scheduled for August. He realized, however, that there was no lack of proven halfbacks returning. Two of them, Al Hall and Billy Martin, were already signed for the pros.

For about a month after the announcement of their engagement everything was fine between Lynne and David. He assured his parents that they need not worry about him obtaining a college degree because he owed it to them, to himself, and most of all to Lynne. He made it plain that 10 years hence he didn't want her to feel sorry because she had married him. He explained that the idea of a wife didn't lessen his ambitions, but heightened them. Furthermore, he was certain that Lynne naturally assumed that he would finish college.

There were all the niceties so dear to the heart of a newly engaged young lady. Apparently very pleased, Lynne's folks wrote to David acknowledging the engagement. Lynne, desperately wanting to be liked, went over to show David's mother her new ring. She wrote to David every day and sometimes twice a day. He, in turn, wrote to her four or five times a week.

But then on May 15 there was a letter from David to his folks with ominous overtones. There was a matter concerning which he evidently found it impossible to be content. He wrote:

> Whatever you do make sure Lynne knows you approve of her. About the only thing you'll find wrong with her is that she's too chubby. But believe it or not, she's got the makings of a figure to match her face. I talked to her on the phone once, and she said she was going to lose some weight. If she does I'll have to be jealous of every man that comes along.

The dike was now breached: the very next day he wrote: "I'm going to write a letter to Lynne getting her to reduce—I think. If I did it right it would be a good thing."

David continued to torture himself with this problem throughout the summer. He was obsessed with the idea of his own unattractiveness to women and was certain in his own mind that, with her pretty face and good personality, Lynne could easily do better than him if she were only to lose some weight. He tried not to worry because he knew it couldn't possibly help; nevertheless, it seemed to him as though his existence had come to an impasse. Like the poet said, his springs of life were poisoned and thinking was confusion. He concluded: "The best I can see is to etch a smile into my face, and with or without Lynne, proceed smilingly to hell."

The whole situation was perplexing and out of it David got the feeling that his life had slipped away instead of being ready to go somewhere. More and more trying to solve the problem made him cynical toward everything. He felt that he was beginning to see what Socrates meant when he said: "All I know is that I know nothing."

Not being able to feel for Lynne what he should, he was beginning not to feel anything, including feeling that there was nothing worth striving for. He wrote to his parents:

Dad has seen my engines run down like this more than once and will be glad to see that I recognize the problem. But this time it seems that the only way to refuel is to get free. Sometimes I wish I had been brought up to be more brutal and callous, then I could put Lynne aside with an easy conscience. Maybe going our separate ways would be nothing more than a slight insult to Lynne. But standing objectively outside myself I see a person who is for some reason timid about insulting those who no one else worries about spitting on. Socrates also said, "Know yourself." If he tried to, no wonder he decided he wasn't sure of anything.

David summed up what he considered to be the heart of what was bothering him the most:

Something's wrong with me and has been for years. Maybe I'm more completely honest with myself than most people. When I was in Los Angeles last week I went to the library and finally found a book I've been looking for on plastic surgery. Maybe I could have an accident to my face and the Marine Corps would pay for repairing

59

it, although it's a very messy process and takes a highly skilled surgeon to do it right. I probably need a psychiatrist. This is the only thing that, really, ever has, does and ever will hurt me. Anything else whatsoever, I feel competent to cope with, but after I look in the mirror I am overwhelmed with a feeling of being lost although I'm not actually ugly. There's no way plastic surgery can make me handsome, but it could make me better looking.

David's mind was occupied with the problem of his feelings toward Lynne when football practice started on August 8, with the first week devoted to calisthenics and drills. David now weighed about 177 pounds and was in excellent shape. As far as he could tell he was the fastest man on the squad although Billy Martin, noted for his speed, was inclined to be lazy so David was willing to put money on himself but couldn't make this claim flatly. He was pleased that for the first time he could recall a coach actually expressed an enthusiastic belief that he was capable of making touchdowns.

But his mental turmoil over Lynne continued. A few days later he wrote her a letter hinting that she lose some weight. He didn't know what her reaction would be, but concluded that it could hardly be pleasant. He feared that it would almost inevitably effect their relationship adversely even if in years to come. But he finally felt that he had to write the letter. When it was sent he was numb. He was all too aware that a girl couldn't help what she thought when a man asked her to marry him, and at the same time stated that she needed to lose weight. It was a touchy matter, he knew, and just didn't set right even though he tried to be casual, tactful, and encouraging. He told her that she had a fine figure so she should lose some weight. He suggested that she should just have her mother feed her fruit and lean meat. He concluded: "Simple. Simple torture. At least it made me comfortably numb for awhile. Who knows what will happen?"

What happened was that David felt remorse for not accepting her as she was and wrote saying that they'd be married the following February after she finished that semester of college. Even then, he felt that he was too young to marry and that to do so was pure folly. But he felt that it was unfair to drag the matter on. He realized that Lynne was no fool and would recognize that further postponing the wedding would only be a dodge. She had sent him a letter almost setting him free, but not quite—almost pleading. Even while suggesting a date, however, he was still uncertain as witnessed by the conclusion of a letter to his parents: "I've lost the horrible feeling that one of us has to be crushed. No matter what happens we may come out a little scarred, but not broken."

Meanwhile, he had been doing so well in football practice that other players were just as shocked as he was when he was cut from the squad on the first day of September. No reason was given for his removal, and he sought none. The probable reason was that the team was riding a 16-game winning streak and was so highly rated that college and service opponents refused to face it. On the team were some of the finest halfbacks in the nation. For David to have broken into this coterie would probably have required a modicum of luck as well as outstanding ability. There was no question about his ability, but when it came to football he had already received numerous convincing demonstrations that he and lady luck had not even a flirting acquaintance.

But being cut from the squad intensified the tension of his engagement to Lynne in a special way. Without the security provided by a place on the regular football team, he faced the prospect of being shipped overseas—probably either Okinawa or Hawaii.

Faced with the probability of two years of duty overseas, David decided that he should offer to release Lynne from their engagement. Lynne wrote back telling David that she knew it would probably be best for him if she let him go, but that she just didn't think she could do it. He now felt sorry and phoned her. Even so, he did not feel that this settled the issue. He concluded a letter to his parents: "I wish I could go to sleep and never wake up: we'll leave the problem for now."

He felt that it might help him with his uncertainties if he were able to see Lynne before going overseas, so he was pleased when her parents financed a trip on October 24-30 to see him. She stayed in a guest house on the base and their visit was pleasant enough, but settled nothing fundamentally.

David had decided on Hawaii over Okinawa for overseas duty so that he could bring Lynne there if they were married and it was possible to do so. He arrived there on December

61

1, 1960, and appreciated the businesslike, military attitude that prevailed there at least in places. But he had been there only a few days when he received what was to him another shock regarding his marriage plans. Lynne mentioned to him in a letter that her folks intended to give them $3,000 for a wedding present. $3,000!! David realized that such a gift would solve a lot of financial problems for them to start out married life, but he reflected that he wouldn't be comfortable around them—or comfortable anywhere—if he accepted such a gift. He wrote to Lynne stating his position.

But then he began to think that perhaps his idealism was foolish. Obviously the money would be very useful to them. He concluded a letter to his parents:

> I wish Lynne could have everything in the world that she could want, and that somebody'd beat me every day until I couldn't stand up. . . I think I'm ashamed of what Lynne's parents want to do for us from listening to other people's tales of hardship, then have something handed to me.

Meanwhile, Lynne was excited and busy with plans for the wedding on February 25, a date David had suggested contingent upon his getting leave on that date. But he learned that March 11 would better fit into the plans for certain battalion maneuvers and made arrangements for leave then. He had to go into the field at once however, and wasn't able to immediately confirm the new date. Lynne, nevertheless, went ahead with the February date, including sending out wedding announcements. When he returned from the field he received a letter from Lynne saying that the announcements had already been sent out, or probably sent out.

David promptly called Lynne to set the matter straight. Lynne had, indeed, already sent out the announcements. When she learned that David had changed the date of his leave she was miserable and almost cried. David knew what the call was costing, but couldn't hang up while she was so unhappy. His mother had recently sent him $30 which went toward the $90 phone bill. Lynne was disconsolate and just didn't see how she could change the date. The next day Lynne called to ask if David had changed the date of his leave. He informed her that he hadn't even tried because it was highly impractical to do so.

On February 25, the date of the original wedding plans, David broke off with Lynne. He had earlier believed that doing so would really hurt her, but events of the past few months had changed his mind. Now he believed that it was not a case of ruining a life as he once had.

David did return to Albuquerque from Hawaii for his leave, however, and he and Lynne reconciled their differences. They were married on March 11, 1961, with Kenneth K. Shook, Rector of All Angels Episcopal church of Albuquerque, presiding. David's brother, Douglas, and Judy Windom witnessed the marriage certificate.

But David was far from reconciled in his own tortured mind. His father sat up with him most of the night before the day of the wedding trying to console him. At times he was entirely incoherent and was obviously as wretched as a human being can be and still survive. His father took the good caution to remove all tools of self-destruction from his presence and finally toward dawn he slept a little.

The wedding was beautiful, with far more people in attendance than were at David's funeral a few short years later. He was composed but his father, particularly, knew the state of his mind only hours earlier and was anxious until the ceremony was over. The reception that evening was joyous. Lynne was absolutely radiant through it all, and David gradually appeared to be more at ease.

On their wedding night David had another fit, not as bad as the one the night before, but bad enough to thoroughly astonish poor, sweet Lynne who didn't know quite what to make of it and David couldn't tell her what was wrong with him. Still, she tried desperately to be very understanding and they both came out of it okay.

On the last day of March David was returning to Hawaii. He and Lynne broke economy by stopping at the mission of San Juan Capistrano and then spent the afternoon at Disneyland which was very crowded since the kids were out of school for Easter. The next afternoon they saw "Spartacus" at the Plantages which was just down the street from Hollywood and Vine. As a finale to their little holiday, David played his violin for Lynne outside in front of their motel. That evening they went to the airport for dinner, but only had time for a snack in the coffee shop. They both had a real good time. And David was keeping a grip on himself with some pills his mother had given him.

David returned to Hawaii and Lynne followed him early

in July with their automobile and other belongings. They were fortunate in being able to live on the base temporarily. Lynne, calling 37 realtors in the process, found a reasonable place for them to live in Kailua—a studio for $75 a month. They were really lucky to find anything, and attributed their good fortune to Lynne's persistence. Most other accomodations, even when available, were $125 and up. They were equally frugal with their other expenditures and to the amazement of aquaintances, managed quite well on David's monthly income.

That fall David encountered his usual bad luck when he tried out for the base football team, and was cut out on the second day of practice. The obvious reason was that the coach had the previous year's championship team back practically intact, and tryouts were only a placatory custom. Also David had been in the field the first day which didn't help get him registered in the coaches all-important first impressions. He had a hint he might be cut when he was the only winner of windsprints not known to the coach by name. Initially he ranged himself against the fastest players he knew and beat them easily (some later made the team). Then, discovering who the really fast ones were, he was ready to go after them (they weren't all running at once or even by position). Although he was sure he could have beaten them all, there were no more windsprints.

Some of the fellows that David had bested in the windsprints were among those he had played with at Camp Pendleton. Being in the coach's company, they were known to him and offered to intercede for David so he returned to practice the next day. The promised overture wasn't made, so David approached the coach himself and asked him to explain his deficiencies as he'd promised to do for anyone who was cut. The coach explained that David had shown a lack of coordination in calisthenics, which was no doubt his standard answer. Of course no one but a cretin can be uncoordinated at basic calisthenics; furthermore, David had shown dexterity in some of the more complex drills such as the back-ward crab and bear walk. More important, such factors are hardly a solid basis for picking a football team.

The coach made it obvious that he hadn't even observed David when he also told him that his speed needed improving. When David informed him that he could run the hundred in 9.7, the coach admitted that he may have cut several players who were good enough for the team, but that he had to do his best and work with the people he knew about. This was a point that David could sympathize with, but didn't console him individually. The coach concluded by saying that if there were enough replacements needed due to injuries and other reasons there would be more tryouts, this time in pads, early in November. David quite justifiably doubted that this would happen.

In December Lynne and David moved to a different apartment. The rent at $80 was five dollars a month more than the old place, but it was much nicer. There was plenty of grass and shrubs with poinsettias and papaya tree in the back. They had enough room so they could have a Christmass tree. There were two distinct rooms and a bath instead of a studio. One was a living room-bedroom and the other a kitchen-dining room. All were nicely furnished, including a full size refrigerator. Also important, there were very few bugs so Lynne was real happy with it. It was also convenient to everything they needed and there was always a nice breeze so David liked it also.

Their first wedding anniversary passed and David showed none of the strain that had characterized his life in the period before they were married. Apparently life was serene both in his marriage and with his work in the Marine Corps.

Early in August Lynne's parents accompanied by her brothers and sisters arrived in Hawaii for a visit. Lynne rented them a small beach house right on the ocean, and they rented a car to transport themselves and their luggage. Lynne ate out with them practically every night, and David did too when he could get off before six. They remained for a week and enjoyed themselves immensely with sunning, swimming, and spear fishing. When they returned home they left their snorkel masks, spear gun, a movie camera and half a bottle of leftover scotch. David and Lynne remained in the rented cottage for one night after her parents left, then returned to Kailua with their new possessions. David wrote to his parents: "I got initiated to wine (quite a cermony they have for serving it) so now maybe I'm ready for the scotch."

Four months earlier, in April, David had requested leave so that he could spend some time with Lynne and her parents during their visit. He was promised this leave all along until the last minute when it was decided that he was needed for inspections. His comrades all knew of this cavalier handling of a promise made and, supposed gleefully that David was taking revenge when he hit a Lieutenant Gorski so hard as to practically knock him unconscious while practicing with pugil sticks. The circumstances warrant explaining. There was a battalion field day and David was selected as his company's representative in the pugil sticks competition. David was reluctant and only volunteered when his platoon was insulted.

He eliminated everyone from the other platoons, then Lieutenant Gorski decided he wanted to spar with him. It was the lieutenant's idea; even so, David later concluded that it hadn't been very diplomatic of him to hit him so often and then knock him down. In the finals David managed to put the eventual winner on his back, although he beat David with more hits.

David was scheduled to be rotated from Hawaii on November 22, so Lynne left for the mainland earlier that month so they would have all of their possessions transported in advance. David followed later and arrived by troop transport in San Francisco on December 10, 1962, picked up his car after a few days wait and then drove to Albuquerque where he was reunited with Lynne. They enjoyed David's leave immensely, but all too soon he was returned to duty in California.

Despite their desire to make a careful selection of as ideal a place as possible, David and Lynne were hounded to bay by the circumstances of his reporting in and had to locate a place quick. The one they selected was the same they had when they were in California earlier. It was okay, but awfully small. Lynne had experienced visions of doing all kinds of wonderful things and being a paragon of domestic virtue and virtuosity, but the place wasn't much to work with and they didn't even have room for everything they brought. Lynne was heartbroken and kept blinking back tears and trying to hide them until David was almost tearful too. David concluded a missive to his parents: "Don't let her find out I told you because she thinks you'll think she's spoiled if you knew. She's okay now and works real hard trying to fix the place up."

March 11, 1963, witnessed Lynne's and David's second wedding anniversary, which David spent on a field problem in the desert at 29 Palms. As if the wind and sand weren't bad enough, it also uncharacteristically snowed. While there he gave out his first traffic ticket, to a staff sergeant speeding in a 6X truck. David told the story:

I'll bet he was furious getting picked up on a dirt

road in the desert miles from nowhere. I know I would
have been. I'd been instructed to give out as many
tickets as possible, but he was the only one I could
catch. He was raising so much dust he couldn't see
me behind him, although the jeep had MP blazoned on
a board across the grill.

David was scheduled for release from the Marine Corps
in September, so in March he started to study university cat-
alogs to see where he would attend school upon his discharge.

# EIGHT

Because of the date of his discharge, David was late in arriving at the University of Montana. He wrote to the dean of admissions saying that he would be a little late for orientation. With gratifying speed the dean wrote back instructing him to just come to his office when he arrived and they would get him in touch with his orientation group and help him catch up to anything he missed.

Early on he decided to forego collegiate athletics and concentrate on his studies, hence he graduated with honors. He did, however, keep himself in excellent condition with weightlifting, running, and hiking in the mountains.

From the beginning it was evident that David would be an unusual student. He was now 23 years old and his naturally inquisitive mind had been broadened by a tour of military duty. Blessed with native intelligence of a high order, he was now ready to intellectually challenge not only himself, but his instructors as well.

He soon learned, however, that his choice of forestry for a major was a mistake. It was not as out-doorsey as he had imagined; furthermore, he found certain aspects that didn't really appeal to him and didn't offset the things that had appealed to him when he started out. After closer contact with the myriad narrowly technological, mathematical subjects (at which he might be competent, but only competent), he began to feel like a square peg in a round hole.

There was a major factor in his change of heart: every time he went to economics class he saw the remains of the charts and work on the board of the previous history class, and it made him drool. After careful consultation with the Testing and Counseling Center he changed back to his original major of history. Ultimately he switched his major to

Spanish and took a number of courses in Russian. He considered that these, along with history, would give him a good background for the diplomatic service which became his ultimate goal.

From the beginning David exercised inconoclastic predilections which generally earned him the approbation rather than censure of his teachers. In the first days when he was struggling with unfamiliar subjects related to his later aborted forestry major, he wrote his parents:

Science text books are funny. They're esoteric before they're sensible or instructive. I can't escape the feeling that deep down inside the authors are afraid that if they present their subject logically, the student will pick it up too easily and the authors will lose their status as little gods of the modern world.

I have one book assigned for chemistry, but purchased four others to supplement it. Using all five I can decode what each one is trying to say. This wouldn't be so bad, except that the process runs to hours and the final message, when deciphered, isn't that complicated. In the meantime the academic year hasn't waited for you.

Anybody contemplating writing a science textbook should be required to hold at least a master's degree in English in addition to his science degree. Then, of course, his book would be in danger of being understood by the less scientifically inclined students. Oh well, the author's ego would just have to suffer.

A little later he expanded this idea:

Maybe it's time for psychology to come to the aid of education, and thereby mankind, by making some advances in the science of semantics. Improvements in the technique of expressing scientific and technical ideas might make it that much easier on the brilliant science student, and enable us all to learn a little more in an alloted amount of time.

Throughout his stay at the University of Montana David got along well with all of his professors. Even so, he never backed off from expressing his own ideas and convictions. He was especially pleased with one "A" that he received from one teacher with a fearsome reputation for severe grading.

On one test he received a grade of 100 while there were a dozen 30's in the class. David concluded that a surprising number of people just didn't give a damn about learning more about their own language, or else they were amazingly stupid.

That English teacher had what might have been some embarrassing moments with David, although he always seemed more puzzled than embarrassed. At any rate they both had sense and humility enough not to crowd one another into a corner. One day David visited the professor in his office and quite cautiously, because he didn't want to antagonize him, doubted the existence of a word he'd been using in class. A search through Webster's unabridged dictionary didn't reveal the word, so David passed off the awkward moment by allowing as how, after all, new words are created from time to time. Another time they differed in class over a passage from a book the teacher was having the class read. In a spirit of cameraderie they wagered a glass of beer on the disputed passage, then shook hands on it.

An examination of the passage revealed that the instructor had been wrong all the time. David's further comment on this potentially jarring exchange helps to reveal why no antagonism was felt on either side.

> The man is an excellent teacher. One of the students who was making only a "D" didn't blame it on the instructor; instead he said the course was the best, most revealing English course he'd ever taken, and felt, despite his "D", that he was really learning something.

Another time David received an "A+" on one of Dr. Sullivan's medieval history tests for nothing more than an explanation in two brief sentences of why he declined to even take the test. This unusual circumstance warrants explanation. Only about a third of the original enrollment survived to take the final examination on the course ("History 208, Coup de Grace," it was jocularly titled at the top of the page). David had taken six of his tests, but had never gotten used to them: the first glance at a new one was like being kicked in the stomach. After he handed in the paper on which he declined to take the test, David was despondent and seriously considered giving up the course. When he saw the "A+" grade instead of the sneering remarks he'd expected, he nearly fell down in the middle of the hall. He told himself that, knowing Sullivan, it was his warped idea of a joke. But later a classmate told David that Dr. Sullivan had showed him the test and confided: "I'd rather have Westphall try and snow me than try and get the straight scoop from someone else."

David's entire test answer said:

> This test is a little too rough for me. In the time allowed I could scatter a little garbage about each item, but I'd just as soon flunk without trying to bluff.

After that test Dr. Sullivan was even more cordial toward David than before, and David never abused this trust. He confided to his parents concerning Dr. Sullivan:

> He gives courses in ancient history which are probably even more interesting than his medieval courses, but I just don't know if my heart could take the strain.

David developed and expressed his political views as he proceeded through his studies, at least in one instance to the sacrifice of an "A" grade. He anticipated that this might happen, although he had a 95 average in political science before the final. But in the final he grew weary of parroting the liberal line as he had done on previous tests and so guessed that his grade might go down.

Indeed it did. He was convinced that his test was fully as good as his previous ones except that on one question he had stopped repeating the left-wing catechism. Here he'd been studying government for two quarters, but hadn't learned a thing about diplomacy when it really counted. He had learned enough about diplomacy to lie all the previous quarter and had enough self-control to lie on every question except one on the final.

He summed up his anti-liberal bias in other ways, as well. Typically:

> If the liberals had to decide who should be shot, Mao Tse-tung or Barry Goldwater, they'd pretend they were thinking for a decent interval, then they'd pick Goldwater. As far as they're concerned he's the more dangerous and sinful of the two. Mao may be responsible for a few deaths and for breaking up a few families in his communes, but nevertheless his approach to gov-

71

ernment is closer to what is "intellectual" and "realistic" than is Goldwater's.

Liberals are always pratting about social justice. (Justice is justice, but what is "social" justice?) None of the personal, pet schemes of MSU professors for implementing "social" justice call for going among the poor and raising them up a notch. They all call for going among the rich and lowering them a notch. They'd quiver with delight, if like mad dogs we'd all turn on capitalism and bite the hand that feeds us. (I saw one prof almost go into ecstacy as he described the nationalization of steel in Britain.) Despite all their plugs for "social" justice I've never seen a liberal prof who sold all his goods to provide for the world's hungry millions, then trudged to school barefoot in the snow wearing a hair shirt. The day I do I'll start to take them more seriously.

He did see more than one side of the political spectrum, but tended to lean toward the right wing. He explained why:

The conclusion I've reached after having my eardrums pierced by shrieks from the left that feudalistic reactionaries are dooming us to stagnation, and by the salvos from the right declaring that radicals, posing as humanitarians, threaten to destroy democracy, is that a democracy, like a bird, can't fly without two wings. However, for various reasons, I lean toward the right wing, and so the majority of professors I've observed appear slightly ridiculous: ever since the days when FDR afforded college professors a new respect and prestige it seems that they've been waiting for a new messiah to appear; when he does all the profs will hurry to Washington where they'll form a new BRAINS TRUST, and taking the reins of what their superior intellects tell them is a logical centrally controlled government, they will save the quivering, down-trodden masses from the nasty Robber Barons, we'll stop our naughty and unreasonable harrassment of the communists, and then we'll live happily ever after in Utopia.

He cited specific and amusing examples of his relations with liberal professors:

There's a midterm in political science Tuesday.

72

It's a very interesting class, but I tend to get a little
weary of the professor's cute jibes at Goldwater. It
seems that professors in general, and political "scien-
itsts" (as they like to call themselves) in particular,
are Democrats. Our political science professor has assured us that his is the more "intellectual" position. He
acutally stood before the class and said that with a con-
ceited smirk on his face. Whereupon I had the temerity
to accuse him of unfair propaganda, which almost turned
his self-satisfaction to apoplexy. Subsequently I went
to see him in his office, and I believe that I've placated
him somewhat. I should have learned to keep my big
mouth shut when last quarter in economics I attacked
labor unions, thereby drawing upon myself the pedagog-
ical wrath. The profs around here shriek about how a
college education makes you open-minded, but just try
and disagree with one of them.

But David was catholic in his interests. He wrote of
another subject:

    In anthropology I've been learning such things as
    that man has a chin and apes don't, probably because,
    while an ape's jaw only goes up and down, man's does
    this and also rotates from side to side and therefore
    man needs the added length of a chin for muscle attach-
    ments and leverage. For some reason I find that kind
    of information spell-binding. When I made the discov-
    ery that my wrist rotates because one of the two bones
    in my forearm can pass over the other one—and not be-
    cause something in my elbow rotates—I must have sat
    for five minutes looking at my forearm, wiggling my
    wrist, and admiring the mechanism I'd carried around
    for twenty-five years without appreciating how it worked.

*      *      *

The first direct knowledge of any impending trouble between David and Lynne was contained in a letter to his parents dated May 20, 1965. He wrote that Lynne and he had
been living in a state of armed truce for the past couple of
months while tolerating each other with an elaborate cour-
tesy. He confided that he was going to New Mexico for the
summer while she was going to continue her courses at the

73

University of Montana.

A great amount of the inner torment that he had suffered
for much of his life from his high school days on now sur-
faced anew. Life became a great weight and an inner com-
pulsion urged him to lay it down. Lynne was suing him for
divorce on the 20th of June. The divorce itself was not devastating to him directly, but it had triggered all of the old
anxieties about his worthiness in the eyes of women. He
was beset with the urge to kill himself.

Lynne didn't seem to be unhappy about the situation;
rather, she viewed it as unfortunate, but one of those things.
She had been living with some friends for some time and her
life was quite occupied with her work in the art department
where she won the award for the outstanding art student of
the year. She had plenty of friends and acquaintances, whereas David had been so totally engrossed in his studies that he
had taken time for little else.

She had journeyed to New Mexico to tell her parents what
she was going to do. Of course they were upset, but took it
very well and graciously. They told her to assure David that
they bore him no ill will and, in fact, wished him good luck.
He, in turn, worried about the reaction of his own parents
and informed them that he was basically as reconciled to the
situation as Lynne was.

David wondered even to himself what had caused all this
and how it had come about. He couldn't say exactly. They
had never really had a quarrel and it seemed to have developed over a period. While he was sure that he wouldn't miss
Lynne, he didn't take the divorce lightly. He had spent a
long time thinking about the religious morality of a divorce
and had studied the pertinent passages in the Bible. He was
aware of the consequences in this regard, but was reconciled.
As for Lynne, her religious ideas didn't seem to have any
scruples about divorce.

But there was more than the divorce of vital concern to
David. He confessed to his parents that he was reaching
the point where he needed help. Lynne had urged him to
see a psychiatrist, and he thought that she was right. The
reasons, as far as David could truthfully determine, were
outside of and basically separate from the pending divorce.
They went back further than his marriage. As stated, he had
a persistent urge to kill himself.

He conceded that no doubt everyone thinks seriously
about suicide at least once in his life, but he couldn't get

the idea out of his mind. When he married Lynne that slowed the urge down for awhile, but it returned with the pending divorce. It was final week and he wrote to his parents that he should be studying, but that for the last two days he'd been sitting in his house sobbing and quaking. He continued:

> I've been pleading with someone to help me so that I can want to live, and since I'm not sure that God is there anymore, I confess my weakness and cowardice to you. I've been begging the walls for so long, I may as well beg where it might help. Writing this is a catharsis, but unless I take steps to defend myself it will come back. When I get to Albuquerque I really think you should help me to see a psychiatrist.

He realized that his position was ridiculous, but realizing it just had never helped. He felt that he had reached the point where to protect either his sanity or his life he had to hold himself up to be ridiculed by the entire world. He realized that most people live unhappy lives, but this was no solace to him and he felt that it was no reason why he should go on submitting to a misery that made him want to trade it in for physical torture. If he could do something to alleviate the misery, which despite being irrational was very real, then he wanted to try. That is why he was asking for help. If he confessed his secret he realized that those who learned it would very possibly despise him, but that if he could be helped that might be better than continuing to despise himself.

He continued with his plea to his parents for help:

> In a word, I'm too ugly for any woman to really love. I do not want to be tolerated. I want to be loved. I think Lynne used to really love me, and that is one of the reasons I seized on her so desperately. I tried very hard to love her, but I never really could. I think that in time she came to realize and accept this, and that is one of the reasons we're being divorced. I do not want to be tolerated the way I tolerated Lynne. I want to be loved. If this is too much to expect out of life, I need help in reducing my expectations. If I'm the victim of some kind of inferiority complex, I need help in escaping it.

75

He continued with as poignant and humbly appealing a plea as can readily be found in writing:

> Maybe all this seems unreal or nonsensical to you. For your sakes I am sorry about the divorce. Possibly I should wait longer than until Sunday for some kind of reply to all this before venturing to come down there, but I'm lonely here. I don't want to upset you, or irritate you, or make you unhappy or anything else, but I don't know what to do about my whole situation except write this.

This was the nadir of David's entire life. From here there could only be either oblivion or rising fortune. To forestall the former, upon receipt of David's letter, his parents immediately departed by automobile from Albuquerque to pick him up in Missoula. They did not then know, nor did he, that after a brief period of readjustment the rest of his life would be marked by an inner calm that transcended all the mental agony of his years as an athlete, student and husband.

## NINE

David's recovery from his despondency was relatively rapid and thorough. Soon after arriving in Albuquerque, with the guidance of his parents, he placed himself under psychiatric care with Dr. Henry W. Blake. In his divorce settlement with Lynne, she had received their car and he the balance of the money in their checking account. David's parents purchased for him a new automobile and this mobility provided a needed boost to his morale. He spent the summer rather leisurely, helping his father with historical research and doing volunteer work in a hospital. David wrote of his psychiatric treatment:

> I'd been married while in the service and was divorced during my last year of school. This crisis brought to a head emotional pressures which had been building for a long time and I consulted a psychiatrist, and underwent a period of psychoanalysis, a very interesting and worthwhile experience. The record of this treatment presented some problems getting into and through Officer Candidate School, but each gamut of "headshrinkers" decided that my psyche was at least as healthy as my body.

Bolstered with the confidence inspired by his psychiatric treatment, he returned to Missoula early in August and worked until school started in September as a laborer in the Missoula White Pine Sash Company. With aid from his parents and veterans educational benefits, he was able to concentrate full time on his studies and earned straight "A's" in a program emphasizing Spanish and Russian.

In order to perfect a working knowledge of Spanish, he

attended summer school at 699 Ramos Arizpe, Saltillo, Coahuila, Mexico. Here he met Irene de la Rosa Fuentes. While David met Irene soon after his arrival in Saltillo, it was August 6 before he asked her for their first date. She was to leave within a few days on a trip to Acapulco and Mexico City before taking up her duties as a school teacher at Monclova some 100 miles north of Saltillo. They parted on August 11, and David started his return journey to Missoula.

An account of their friendship is beautifully and poignantly told in five letters, translated from the original Spanish, written to David by Irene after he returned to school in Montana. They speak eloquently and universally of devotion and love:

My adored David, when seeing the moon it reminded me of you, since it was the same moon you saw each night. . . . Thank you so much for the flowers you sent before you left. I also liked the two owls you sent me. I have them with me today in Monclova. Barbon and Florisponro are next to me sitting on top of the donkey. . . . You have inspired me to have confidence, love and admiration from the day when we first met. . . . I realize I am jealous, and I also do not wish to share you with anyone (not even Juanita). . . . You write and express yourself well in Spanish and I am happy that you are pleased with the gifts I sent you. Please answer soon. . . . All I have thought of is your returning since you first left. . . . Even if I did not have a photo of you, I would always remember you as handsome as you were when you were here. I have three photos of you and you look very handsome in all of them. . . . With your letter were enclosed the postcards. They are indeed very beautiful and I showed them to my roommates who agree to their beauty. . . . Once again I compliment your playing the guitar and thank you for the song you wrote for me. . . . You tell me you are going to Quantico, VA. Am I given to understand you are going to some camp? Could this be because of the war and the existing problems abroad? I hope you will still be coming in December. . . . I hope that someday I can personally thank you for your generosity. Hopefully this will be in December (could this be in December?). I ask you because your letters indicate you might come in December. . . . Should you decide to come in December I shall be happy to have you here and to be at your side. . . . My feelings for you have not changed; they are and will always be the same. I am sure that you know all this and that Katy has reassured you of my feelings for you. . . . May you receive this letter with all the love enclosed for you from your girl who thinks of you always. . . . I remember just for an instant that you were so happy this made me happy since there were a few times you were so serious and just a little bit unhappy. I shall never forget every moment we were together. . . . I remember the 6th of August, the first time you asked me for a date. It was such a happy time for me but also sad because I knew you would be leaving soon. I was afraid I would never see you again, but you see such is our destiny that I shall see you again and very soon. . . . It was inevitable that we somehow finally sought each others company. . . . It is quite strange that one person can understand the other by a simple correspondence of a letter (not only strange but beautiful). It is my wish that you write to me telling me of your thoughts, your likes and dislikes, share them with me. Everything that concerns you is of interest to me. . . . I consider our friendship very special, like an illusion, a beautiful dream, where one person meets another, where you love and understand and there are no faults only love and in the end like a beautiful poem. He who loves the most forgives and gives the most. . . . These expressions on my part are small next to yours. Even if our love is inexperienced two people who love each other, confide and have respect for each other, will find each other. . . . Everything that is good is beautiful and the affection two people have for each other is the most beautiful of all. Love endures separation and sadness through memories of each other. . . . I do hope my thoughts are not too simple and that you will think about what I have said. I leave you with all my love.

Irene

*       *       *

David finished his final quarter toward a degree on December 13, 1966, with an A grade in all subjects. He graduated with honors that following June, although he was unable to attend the graduation exercises.

He was offered a graduate assistantship by the foreign language department of the University of Montana to work on his M.A. degree, but decided in favor of rejoining the Marine Corps as an officer. At the time that he made his decision the United States had 385,000 men in South Vietnam and was irretrievably committed there. Many young men were looking for ways to avoid military duty because of the specter of possible service in Vietnam. By contrast, David had already honorably served in his nation's armed forces and there could not be even a hint that he owed more. Still, when he was offered employment leading to an advanced degree in the field of languages that he had come to love, he turned it down in favor of further military duty. Why? Basically, he thought that the line must be drawn somewhere against the spreading threat of world Communist domination. He viewed this challenge as a task calling for voluntary dedication, and was willing to do his part. He wrote: "My fellow citizens pay the taxes to support me, and I intend to be worth the pay."

As matters developed he was to give even his life to earn his pay. And beyond that, his entire Marine Corps career was devoted to excellence. Time after time he performed uncomplainingly duties over and beyond what might be expected of him. His only complaint was the sloth and incompetence of certain of those with whom he came in contact. His only bitch was against the grumblers and complainers who sought to lighten their load along the way. His only gripe was for those who habitually sought the easy path.

David had planned another trip to Mexico to visit Irene right after he finished school in December, but was delayed until January 1967. On the way he stopped to see his parents who had, meanwhile, purchased Val Verde Ranch in northern New Mexico and moved there. His visit with Irene and his other friends in Saltillo was delightful, and even included a trip to Mexico City where he was invited to a wedding. He almost got stuck in the capital when northern Mexico had its biggest snow in 95 years, but managed to get back without mishap.

Evidently David corresponded with Irene after he went to Vietnam for he mentioned her to some of his friends, but the nature of their relationship cannot be determined because his personal papers and letters were never returned to his parents. Despite deligent efforts to locate Irene in Mexico, her whereabouts there could not be learned.

He spent a few interesting days in Washington before

reporting down to Quantico, Virginia, on January 23 for the 43rd officer candidate class. The class was to run to March 31. After having already been through so many training camps he knew that the inspections would be a pain, but there would be a day and half off every week so it wouldn't be like boot camp. He soon learned that about 90 per cent of the instructors were veterans of Vietnam and a majority of them had purple hearts.

David was commissioned on March 22, 1967. Of the 824 candidates who started the course 573 finished. Of these he ranked eleventh so he easily qualified for a regular commission. A new phase of his life had begun and he intended to make the most of the next five months at basic school. Soon after the start of the course he put in for infantry duty in Vietnam and was almost certain of getting it.

What pleased him most about his instruction was that of the three areas that comprised a total lineal standing—academic, leadership, and military skills—he was first in his platoon in military skills. He considered this to mean nothing more than that he was an expert private, which he should have been after his previous four years of experience. He was still rusty at subjects like map reading and technique of military instruction, but was pleased with his progress in general since while privates make war with rifles, machine guns, and mortars, lieutenants make war with radios, maps, and men.

The last weeks passed quickly. Because of high ranking in his class, he was listed for subsequent duty as a reconnaissance platoon commander. Before going overseas he was scheduled for a two or three week school at Camp Pendleton and then probably more training at Okinawa or in the Phillippines. His duty assignment was to the 3rd Marine Division. It was a real honor to be assigned to recon. All the enlisted men in reconnaissance units were volunteers and the junior officers selected were considered the best in the Marine Corps.

On August 29, 1967, his brother, Douglas, came from the University of Indiana at Bloomington to watch David graduate from Basic School. They then drove to their parents' home at Val Verde in their respective cars, arriving there together on September 2. Douglas had to leave on the tenth to register for his next semester and David stayed on at Val Verde.

He enjoyed nearly a month at Val Verde busying himself with the activities that he enjoyed—reading, hiking in the woods, chopping wood—simple pleasures that provide unfeigned relaxation.

But he also challenged himself with more difficult tasks. One of these was to test his mettle as a combat Marine by hiking in a direct line from Val Verde across the wilderness of tangled growth and successive ridges and valleys to a point midway up the formidable southeast flank of Wheeler Peak, the highest point in New Mexico. He was accompanied on this foray by the family dog, Anna, and the going was so rugged that oftentimes he was compelled to help her along the way. He returned weary, but elated by the physical prowess that had enabled him to accomplish what few would even contemplate much less attempt.

Since he had not gone all the way to the top of the peak, and wanted to do so, his father accompanied him there a few days later. But this time they went by Jeep to the base of the mountain where they intersected a well-made trail. On the way they became stuck in a marsh where even four-wheel drive provided inadequate traction. They were compelled to scrounge brush to place under the jacked up wheels in order to extricate their vehicle literally a foot or two at a time. Since they had sailed along blithely unaware of their predicament for many yards through treacherous going before finally bogging down, it took them nearly the whole day to liberate their vehicle.

Since the day was nearly ended and they had brought sleeping bags for just such an emergency, they stayed there the night camping under the stars. They talked for some little time, but their exertion had wearied them so they soon slept soundly until the first light of the new day. Even by trail, climbing the 13,161 foot peak required no small exertion. The high point of the hike was looking far down a precipitous slope upon Blue Lake, a sacred place of the Taos Pueblo people. From their high vantage point the lake appeared as a jewel of the deepest blue clasped in a setting of exquisite sylvan beauty in a steeply walled and heavily forested bowl. The day was clear but crisp with the portent of winter already in the air at that altitude. They did not tarry long at any one location, but could view their shining blue beauty from many locations along the trail.

While at the time David's father had no presentiment that this would be their last time together alone, he savored the occasion to the fullest. It would be difficult to imagine a more unblemished setting for a last long visit with one's eldest son who would soon be off to war. The time was not

82

festive, of course, but neither was it as somber as it might have been had either of them suspected the rancorous cancer that the war in Vietnam would soon hurl precipitately into the bowels and souls of their nation of people.

True, as early as 1964 there had been rumblings of discontent over the war. That year folk singer Bob Dylan skyrocketed in popularity with songs protesting the hypocrisy of American society, while Democratic Senators Ernest Gruening of Alaska and Wayne Morse of Oregon registered the first congressional opposition to the Vietnam War. The subterfuge of the Gulf of Tonkin Resolution of August 7, and the resulting expansion of United States military involvement, caused increasing civil discontent and demonstrations against the war through 1965 and 1966, and congressional opposition was intensified under the leadership of Senator J. William Fullbright.

Now it was 1967, and antiwar demonstrations increased both in strength and virulence. In October Florence Beaumont, a 56-year-old California housewife, burned herself to death in front of the Los Angeles Federal Building in protest against American Vietnam involvement. She was one of seven Americans who chose this grisly form of protest. But it would be 1968 before the floodgates of opposition were opened and the divisiveness in our society became apparent. The January 30 "Tet Offensive" shattered any belief among most politicians and the public alike of any United States military victory in Vietnam. This was the real impetus that began the irreparable convulsion of American society.

As David's father looked back later, although there was no mention of it then, he could see signs that David, unconsciously or otherwise, knew that he would not return alive. As the September 28 departure date approached he made preparations for leaving. These included making initial arrangements toward the sale of his Datsun sports car. His parents would complete the details after he left. He was insistent that this be done. But the most significant indication of such a premonition had its roots in an event of his early youth.

When his father was serving in the South Pacific during World War II, David's mother purchased for him a book entitled WINGS FOR PER. This book was his favorite childhood possession. It could not then be known that he would one day serve his country in the war in Vietnam, and that his last official address and home would be Val Verde Ranch near

Eagle Nest, New Mexico, in the foothills of Wheeler Peek, highest point in the State.

Prior to his departure for Vietnam, David designated a number of his books as a gift to the local school library. His last action before going to the bus on his way to Vietnam was to bring WINGS FOR PER to his mother and say: "I can't give this book, it is worth a million other books."

The conclusion of WINGS FOR PER reads: "Then I will fly up into the clear, washed air of spring and soar over the eagle's nest and over my home under the crag. Mother will stand in front of the house and clasp her hands in wonder. She will say: 'Look, Per has wings.'"

But there was nothing especially significant about the twenty-five mile trip by car to Taos to meet his bus. He and his parents were early as was their wont. There was no attempt to either evade or make light of the grim nature of his leave-taking to a field of potentially mortal danger. Nor was there any pretensions of levity to gloss over the seriousness of the business at hand. At the last moment before he had to board his bus, he embraced his mother with one arm while his father held his other hand in both of his and said: "Take care of yourself and your men." He replied: "I will," and he was gone. They would never see him again, not even in death for his coffin was sealed.

He was processed in at Camp Pendleton for two weeks further training beginning on the 9th. There he met Captain Rocky Wirsching, who was to play an important part in his life for the next several months. Captain Wirsching, a graduate of the Naval Academy at Annapolis had spent the first 15 months of his Marine Corps career after Basic School at Quantico, Virginia as a student jet aviator. He was dropped from the flight program shortly before he would have received his wings because he couldn't pass the final eye exam. He was offered the back seat in a F-4 Phantom jet, but if he couldn't fly as a pilot he preferred the Marine ground forces. A usual requirement for a recon officer was much prior infantry experience. While he had none, he was a good athlete and an excellent swimmer; besides, he was very emphatic in requesting recon duty. He chose the infantry MOS and was assigned to the 2d Recon Battalion at Camp Lejeune, North Carolina.

When David met him, Rocky had just completed 16 months there. Earlier he had made a Mediteranian cruise as a recon platoon commander. His varied background had made him very adept and knowledgeable of the strengths and weaknesses of a grunt company.

Rocky and David were both assigned to a special training course entitled "Recon Officer Supporting Arms." The training was very intensive and demanding. The instruction related to such items as the control of air strikes, artillery, and naval gunfire. Since Rocky had been in recon and David had been earmarked for that billet, both assumed that they would be going to a reconnaissance unit in Vietnam.

They soon became firm friends. Rocky was 26 years old and David a year older. Rocky was a captain with more extensive officer training, while David was a lieutenant with a valuable background as an enlisted man. They spent many of their free evenings together at the officers' club exchanging thoughts and ideas over a cold brew. Rocky was impressed with David's maturity and depth of mind.

There were about 30 men in that special training class, and fewer than half returned from the war. Rocky's roommate was killed as was David—his best friend. But then they were a proud, defiant bunch; no challenge was beyond their reach.

By October 24 they had completed their special training which was "pretty good" except their class never got the jets it was supposed to have to practice with on that day. They left Camp Pendleton and went to Norton Air Force Base in San Bernardino. Here David trimmed his baggage from 135 pounds to 75 pounds in expectation of a flight to Okinawa that evening. From there they would proceed to Vietnam. David's last stateside roommate had been a "most interesting" Catholic Chaplain.

Fatefully there happened to be a typhoon at Okinawa so their departure was delayed for three days. In the tradition of young Marines they threw a departure party on their last night in the states which would be long remembered by the Air Force. The Air Force officers became up tight as the Marines corraled the available women for the evening for themselves. One guy tried to pick a fight with Captain Wirsching in the men's room. He accused Wirsching of stealing his girl, and lost his argument violently. Later David remarked to his buddy that an Air Force officer had to be pretty dumb to pick a fight with a Marine. And the Marines were left alone for the remainder of the evening to enjoy their merriment and fun.

Their departure from the states was very hung-over.

Heads were just beginning to clear when there was a three hour refueling layover at Hawaii which provided an opportunity for another celebration. This time the officers and enlisted men tied one on together. This one was marked by especially abrupt downing of the spirits that cheer because they would soon be off again toward Vietnam. Rocky joked to David that this surely had to be a screwed up war the way they were flying to it in a Braniff Airlines crazy colored airplane with stewardesses dressed in psychedelic attire. After all, weren't Marines supposed to go to war assaulting across beaches or charging out of helicopters?

They landed in Okinawa early in the morning and were sent to processing which included checking in their stateside belongings—items which were almost certain to be eternally lost in the vast base storage and supply facility. They all got their gamma globulin shots in the butt with a needle that would make a horse wince. From there it was up the hill to the officers' club for their final bash and the consumption of pain killer to ease the ache where they sat down.

The next day was mount out to Vietnam, that long anticipated experience where each would withdraw to his own inner thoughts. Soon they would arrive and the remembrance of the togetherness of the past few days would fade as they went to their individual destinies—each to his own direction as leaves in the wind.

They landed at Danang airfield just in time to watch a Marine F-8 Crusader airplane come screaming down the runway, make a gear up landing, and slide off the end of the runway and burn. The pilot popped his canopy and departed the scene as though propelled by the winged heels of Mercury. David remarked laconically: "Some arrival show they scheduled for us."

TEN

David and Rocky Wirsching arrived in Danang on the last day of October, 1967. They went immediately to "arrival" processing, a dumpy little shack located in squalid isolation on the edge of the airfield. The assignments officer was a major who looked tired, tired as does a man who has for too long been the orchestrator of fighting men's destinies. He wore his troublesome worries as though they were a crown of thorns.

Both David and Rocky expected to be assigned to the 1st or 3d Recon Battalion, Rocky because he was an experienced recon officer and David because he had been scheduled for that duty after completing his basic training. As it happened though, the day before their arrival Bravo Company, 1st Battalion, 4th Marines had been ambushed and badly shot up while on patrol in the foothills west of Camp Evans. Camp Evans was located about 50 miles northwest of Hue on the edge of the coastal mountains between Phu-Bai and Quang Tri, 20 miles south of the D M Z.

When they met the assignments officer, Rocky was the only 0302 (infantry officer) to replace the wounded company commander of Bravo Company. He was told immediately that this would be his assignment. He had not expected this at all. He was a recon grunt; the super-spook type who traveled only in small patrols behind enemy lines. He had never been in an infantry company; now he must face the challenge of commanding one. David was former enlisted infantry and wanted to go with Rocky. And Rocky wanted David because they were friends; furthermore, David's infantry experience would be helpful. The personnel officer declined their mutual request because the 4th Marines was supposed to get a captain but no lieutenant that day.

Neither Rocky nor David made any effort to conceal their displeasure. The major, seeing their agitation and the evident bond of friendship between them, relented to their wishes. Perhaps he sensed that they would be a good team together.

Now they had a little time to themselves and learned that the Marines were everything they were cracked up to be on the approaches to the battlefield: boozing, wenching, swaggering—just like in the movies. David added in a letter to his parents: "Soon enough I'll find out about the battlefield, too."

Later that day they caught a ride on a C-130 to Phu-Bai. As they tried to sleep that first night in Vietnam they were constantly awakened by the thunder of the incessant outgoing H & I artillery rounds. This booming was soon to become commonplace.

Early the next morning they hitched a ride in a convoy of trucks enroute from Phu-Bai to Camp Evans. They could have ridden in a chopper, but elected to go with the convoy so that they could go through Hue. This was their first look at the Vietnamese people, the battered countryside, and the rolling coastal plain.

David wrote of the people:

> Some of the women have a quiet, serene kind of beauty. . . The kids, and they come in hordes—I guess because most of them don't go to school— are extremely cute little beggers (literally), but they grow up to be very ugly adults. Most of the Marines here despise them, and it would be easy to let yourself be disgusted by them.

At Camp Evans Rocky met the Battalion CO and was informed that he was now the Bravo Company commander. He asked that David be assigned to his company and his request was granted.

The old man, the Battalion CO, who had been a platoon commander in Korea, was less than effective in the command of his battalion. As a field commander in the jungle he was far behind the times.

The Battalion XO was a giant of a man who had been Rocky's boxing coach while he was a midshipman at the Naval Academy. He was tediously loud and overbearing in demeanor, but remembered Rocky from their Academy days and put in a good word for him to the Battalion Commander. The CO had been plagued with some bad experiences with recon Marines in Korea and he was apprehensive when Captain Wirsching informed him that all of his experience was with recon patrols—that he had never served in an infantry unit. Obviously, he would be keeping a close eye on Bravo Company. Rocky told the CO that David was good—a real hotshot lieutenant— who had earlier served in the 4th Marines as an enlisted man.

Later that day they met Bravo Company, or what was left of it. Fourteen Marines were killed and many more wounded. Every officer except the 2d lieutenant then commanding was wounded. All the staff NCO's except one were also hit, as well as the radiomen and the hospital corpsman who had gone to the aid of the wounded. The ambush of the company would have been much worse had not a quick thinking gunnery sergeant found a working radio over which he called for and obtained emergency suppressive fire from a Huey gunship just in the nick of time. The ambush had been well prepared on a jungle trail in the mountains. The surviving troops related how deadly it had been—a real disaster.

David had known three of the wounded lieutenants from basic school. Two were returned to the states, and the third returned to Camp Evans "still picking shrapnel out of his chin." One young private, who had only been in Vietnam three days, was in the ambush. David candidly reported: "He went berserk, kind of like me on my wedding night." He then corrected the sentence to read: "kind of like me on the eve of my wedding day," and added, as a postcript: "That corrected sentence up there was a lulu before I corrected it."

David had, indeed, been upset on the day before his wedding. He had a fixation about his facial appearance. His nose, unlike most noses, slanted essentially from his forehead without the usual more or less indented bridge. Having had it broken several time in football hadn't helped. Actually, it was entirely normal in appearance which he usually admitted, but at times he considered it ugly and feared that no woman could really love him because of it. Just before his wedding was one of the periods during which he was depressed about this feature of his facial appearance.

Company morale was at a rockbottom low. The troops all had the feeling that it would only be a matter of time before they got theirs; few believed that they would ever make it home. The Company XO had not been in the field at the time of the ambush. The only surviving officer was one 2d lieutenant who was very new at his job; in fact, he had been in Vietnam for only three weeks. He tried hard, but was an unfinished product of the officer factory.

Captain Wirsching was grateful that David was in his company and assigned him to the command of the first platoon. By chance, from 1960-1962, he had been literally a private in the rear rank of the same platoon and company of the 4th Marines while on duty in Hawaii. He felt that he had really good material to work with and was frank in his judgement that how good it turned out to be depended on what he did with it.

There was one symbol around which to rally the morale of the dispirited company. First Sergeant Thomas McKinney had the guidon for B-1-4 which had its origin in World War II days. When David first saw it he did his best to acquire it for his own. This he never did during his lifetime, but some years after his death Sergeant McKinney presented it to David's father to be the property of the Vietnam Veterans Memorial Chapel.

The whole company was a mass of disorganization. Captain Wirsching told the company gunny to fall in the company on the road. What a zoo that was. Finally everybody was found. The new replacements were apportioned as needed to fill in the vacancies, squads were formed, fire team leaders assigned, and all organizational details were completed. The captain then ordered a rifle inspection. It was not a formal one, but it was his first chance to meet the men of his command.

Later that day Captain Wirsching went to the Battalion C.P. for the daily staff meeting. The tactical assessment of the operation in which Bravo Company had been decimated was presented. The company had been proceeding on a trail in the mountain jungle when it was ambushed. The battalion knew that the NVA were on the hill before they went there— the NVA were still there. Nothing was gained. The operation had been conducted like war games only with live ammo! It stunk!

That evening he had to write personal letters to the parents of the marines who had died in the ambush—a most sobering experience. Since he knew none of these men, he interviewed most of the men in the company who had been there to obtain details about the lives of their fallen comrades. He learned a great deal that evening and came away wondering how the previous company commander could have been dumb enough to travel on a trail. Absolutely asinine!

90

David did a hell of a job that night. By morning his platoon was well on its way to being organized, while the others were still fumbling around. That day was spent just getting equipment in shape and generally finding themselves again.

The next day Bravo Company was going on its first mission following the ambush. Hopefully contact with the enemy would be light for they were still untested as a unit. The elements of command, the unity of the company, was still very weak. Again that night there was very little sleep for Rocky and his lieutenants. His first understanding with the company was that he would not tolerate the expression: "That's the way we always did it before." He told the men a little of his own background then informed them that David had been an enlisted man in Bravo 1-4 several years earlier.

Captain Wirsching then delivered the most important part of his morale building speech. He told the men: "It will be a cold day in hell when I let you get ambushed and shot up stupidly again. Trust your officers as we trust you and no dumb slant-eyed son of a bitch will ever beat us. We are going to do our thing and I'll be damned if the jerks who run our battalion will stupidly interfere."

Captain Wirsching organized Bravo Company differently than the standard Marine infantry company. The usual practice is three rifle platoons and a weapons platoon in a company. He deemed it better for the situation at hand to farm out the machine guns and 60mm mortars to the platoons rather than keep them under his direct control. This would give each platoon more firepower organic to itself, which was better because the terrain and the rice paddies created situations where each platoon was usually on its own anyhow.

None of the officers or NCO's were to ever wear rank insignia outside of the base camp; these made it too easy to recognize a command group at a distance. The enemy knew that officers and certain other ranks were assigned a pistol as a weapon. To confuse the identity of these persons everyone in Bravo Company would carry a rifle to the field except for platoon commanders and sergeants who were to carry shotguns. The shotgun is very effective in close combat, but primarily this weapon was to be an identifying badge of rank. All pistols, if any, were to be carried in a place of concealment because the black pistol holster hanging from the belt was a dead give away that the wearer was someone of importance. Eventually only fire team leaders and above could wear a mustache (this explains why David wrote home for mustache wax). This inconspicuous device was an effective way to determine rank within the company. All radios were to be camouflaged in the back pack with the handset hidden in a green sock suspended from the helmet. When needed everyone was required to paint their face green, thus Bravo Company never lost a man to a sniper. The whole concept, as Captain Wirsching explained in great detail to the company, was to confuse the enemy as to the organization of Bravo Company.

The mission of Bravo Company's first patrol following the ambush was to see what was out southwest of Camp Evans, an area near where the company had been ambushed the week before. This was the beginning of an intended operational sweep around Hue. Spirits were high as David led his platoon across the first rice paddy. First platoon had point; the varsity always plays the toughest games.

From the outset the change in the faces and attitudes of the troops was apparent. There would be no more dumb, stupid mistakes like walking down trails or along the crest of rice paddy dikes. They were going where the enemy would not expect them to be, so no more booby traps. They registered their big guns of supporting artillery on the tree line on the other side of a rice paddy before moving out in the open to cross it. David was a real tiger, careful to never expose himself or his men needlessly. He knew how green the company was and moved forward with deliberate advance.

Toward the end of the first day they had gone five or six miles from Camp Evans when they encountered their first hostile fire. A sniper on a hilltop started to spray the advancing formation with semi-automatic rifle fire. For the first time David heard the characteristic chug-chug-chug of a Russian AK-47 assault rifle and deployed his troops quickly. He had one fire team return the fire and had his 60mm mortar fire white phosphorous at the position to mark it. Rocky knew from the location of the sniper that he couldn't see David's men, so told David to hold his fire. There might have been many more of the enemy than just the lone sniper. If David didn't reveal his position or deployment there was little likelihood that he would be attacked in force; furthermore, he was in an excellent position to cover the rest of the company as it hurriedly exited from the open expanses of the rice paddies. No one panicked and went on the paddy dikes, just the uniform coordinated movement from the open to the protection of the tree line. The other lieutenants were also doing their job well.

One of the troops fell crossing a rice paddy dike. He broke his back and was in agonizing pain. His comrades radioed for an emergency medevac helicopter and were informed that it would not arrive until a gunship could be found as an escort since they were receiving hostile fire at the time. This was Captain Wirsching's first taste of battalion staff bullshit. He yelled for his artillery forward observer, Sergeant Rhoen, the "Cowboy," as he was called. Rocky told him to take off the top of the hill on which the sniper was located. About three minutes later 18 rounds of 155 mm high explosive artillery arrived and at once removed the top of the hill.

Later he was chewed out by the Battalion CO for using so much artillery on one sniper, but he didn't give a damn. They got their helicopter and removed their injured man; besides, it was a hell of a good show for the men of Bravo Company indicating that their leader meant business. Even more important, it was imperative that the company not remain static for very long. The NVA had many mortar positions in the overlooking hills. As long as there were only a few Marines visible at a time, and if they kept moving and remained well spread out, there was a good chance that the enemy would not waste their precious ammo on such chancy targets. They had to carry all of their ammo over the mountains on their backs.

Their first night in the field was relativey uneventful. They spotted movement through their starlight scope, but battalion would not give them permission to fire on it. This was the first of numerous frustrating examples where they were denied permission to shoot at the enemy for one stupid-ass reason or another.

The next day they continued their patrol with David always at the point. The day was uneventful. Some VC took a few potshots at them and they shot back, but the score was still no hits, no runs, no errors.

Each morning the Cowboy would faithfully register the guns of the artillery battery which was supporting them. He could tell if a gun was firing a bit long and would give the battery hell until they had the error corrected. The company air controller, also a sergeant, was a real pro. Captain Wirsching never had to ask his FO about his supporting arms. He always had the answers: how much, how soon, and how good they were.

And then the rains came. The moonsoon was miserable.

Fatigue was beginning to set in. David's platoon encountered more VC snipers, but again drove them off. The company headed back toward Camp Evans. Everyone was feeling really miserable. David described his own wretchedness. His feet were beginning to bleed from being constantly wet, his hands were a mass of red welts from thorn cuts, his face was swollen from mosquito bites, he had a rash on his legs where the leaches had bitten him, and his flak jacket was biting into his shoulders where it was pulled down even tighter by a pack which included extra machine gun ammo and mortar rounds. He was trembling with cold and had diarrhea. For an instant he thought he'd throw down all his gear, slump into the water of the rice paddy, and sob.

Little creeks and streams they had waded across earlier were now raging torrents. They tried to ford the streams using rubber ladies (the Marine's name for air mattresses). There were about 200 men in the company with 180 in the field. It took an hour to cross the first stream with six men and another hour to cross them back when it became apparent that the task was hopeless. They were in effect stranded, only eight miles from Camp Evans, but nevertheless stranded. Finally they found a little higher ground, not dry gound, but higher than that over which they had been wading for the past few days. Immersion foot was becoming serious. The platoon commanders reported several cases of severe bleeding immersion foot. David's platoon had nine men temporary casualties from this malady.

Rocky called Battalion HQ and requested that immediate arrangements be made to airlift them out. He at once got a ration of crap from the Battalion CO to the point that they were Marines and that they should be able to walk back. Rocky couldn't believe what he was hearing. The Colonel finally got off the radio and he asked to speak to the XO, who knew Rocky well and who listened. Captain Wirsching flat out told him that they weren't a bunch of ducks; that they had many bad cases of immersion foot and that they were OK but stuck. He added that if they were ordered to march back they would be out of action for weeks as a company, and that there was a damn good possibility of drowning some good Marines in crossing the streams.

Later that day the entire company was airlifted back to Camp Evans by two H-34 helicopters flying several sorties. The troops with the worst feet went first. They were a sorry lot. The day was November 10, 1967, the USMC birthday, and Bravo Company arrived wet, sick, and too late for any food—not even a piece of the traditional cake. But none complained for Bravo Company came back intact as a unit. True, the rains, the leeches, the gooks, the cold, the misery were there, but they had sustained no combat casualties —no booby traps or the like. Rocky expected to be dumped on all over by the Battalion CO, but he said only a few words. Perhaps he could see in the faces of the troops that they were proud. They had given their all to make Bravo Company work again.

That evening Captain Wirsching held an officers' meeting. David was the old pro and was respected as such. Rocky's younger lieutenants had lost their college glow and were now committed to their jobs and the welfare of their men.

Captain Wirsching had inherited one real gem with Bravo Company—1st Sergeant Thomas McKinney who had served for 22 years in the Marine Corps in the infantry MOS. He knew all of the back door tricks of getting things with no questions asked as does only a really superlative 1st sergeant. He reserved the important documents for the captain's signature, but he could sign his commander's name perfectly for everyday routine administrative BS that somehow always manages to follow into a combat situation.

And Sergeant McKinney was good in the field. The afternoon while two choppers were shuttling the company back to base camp when it was stranded by high water, some VC snipers opened up on their position. They were coming damn close; however, to have used artillery on them might have screwed up the helo lift. The company was dug in so Captain Wirsching decided to let the troops deal with the snipers. One young machine gunner opened up on the VC position shooting John Wayne style rather than with accurate, coordinated, effective bursts. This was too much for Sergeant McKinney who jumped out of his hole, ran across the hilltop oblivious to the sniper fire directed at him, and scrambled into the hole with the young machine gunner. He then irately commenced to beat the hell out of the Marine for abusing his machine gun.

Once the 1st sergeant had gained the Marine's attention he masterfully proceeded to instruct him in the routine of properly firing his weapon. Timed bursts of four or five rounds at a time, watch your sights, watch your target, THINK. When the 1st sergeant left that position Bravo Company had one damn good machine gunner. He either got the

95

VC or they called it quits. Another good Marine had joined the team. For this act of heroism Sergeant McKinney was later awarded the Navy Commendation Medal.

The next few days were spent in the relative quiet and safety of the sanctuary at Camp Evans training, and regrouping. At the daily battalion staff briefing Rocky was informed that on November 13 they would go on a heliborn assault into the mountains about 25 miles southwest of Camp Evans. Initial information was vague; the only entlightenment he received was that Bravo Company would be in the assault wave. He had his platoon commanders drill and rehearse their men accordingly.

This mission must have been unique in the annals of Marine Corps history. Only a regimental staff officer who had spent his time managing Disneyland could have devised a more ridiculous assignment. Their charge was to conduct a heliborn assault and land on a remote bend of a river far back in the jungle mountains to seize a supposed large cache of VC rice which was reported to be hidden in caves in the cliffs overlooking the river. The plan may have seemed feasible on the maps in the command bunkers wherein the daily reams of useless paper work originated, but in the field it was a monstrosity of miscalculation.

Two days before the scheduled assault Rocky boarded a helicopter along with several other key officers in the battalion for a supposedly clandestine overflight of the landing area. It seemed awful dumb to him to overfly the landing area, thus revealing their intentions.

Bravo Company prepared intensively for the assault. Traditionally the company commander briefed his platoon commanders who in turn briefed their troops. Captain Wirsching deemed this method to be inadequate right then because, except for David, he was not confident that his platoon commanders would do a thorough job; consequently, he had the briefing attended by all men who held the position of squad leader or above. He spun out the concept of the operation, explaining the pros and cons, strengths and weaknesses, and courses of action to be taken in case of a major screwup, or if the LZ became too hot to land the remainder of the battalion and they were left to fight it out on their own. He asked questions of the men until everyone understood every requirement.

H-hour was scheduled for 0800, an hour or so after daybreak. During the final briefing Captain Wirsching had the squad leaders, platoon commanders, and platoon sergeants all form a circle which represented their perimeter defense after their landing and exit from the landing zone. The captain went around and around the circle until each squad leader knew exactly who was on his left, his right, and where each platoon and the company CP was to be located. If the action became hot there would be no time for orders, only the continuity of remembered directions and assignments.

The objective was a small peninsula formed by a southward bend in the river which flowed from the west toward the sea. On the east side a small sandy beach constituted the LZ, which was surrounded on all sides by very steep cliffs. To visualize, one might think of looking at a tiny spot in the bottom of a bucket. They would be sitting ducks cavorting on the lowest terrain around, and with precious little cover. Even more disturbing, there would be no artillery support except for possibly the very inaccurate and sometimes wayward high angle fire from the big guns. And much of the target area was on the reverse slopes unreachable by artillery.

Directions for egress from the LZ were simple, and were throughly covered in the preassault briefing of the company. Those troops who were assigned to the east beach, as they looked out across the river, would be looking into the sun; those on the south or tip of the peninsula would have the sun on their left shoulder; those on the west would have the sun at their backs. The assignment of conventional directions such as east or west would have been meaningless.

The weather was clear on the morning of the assault. Everyone was up early and ready to go. There were eight H-34 helicopters in the assault wave, each carrying four combat equipped infantry Marines. Captain Wirsching was in the fourth chopper so as to arrive in the middle of the LZ. David was in the first chopper because his assignment was the west edge of the peninsula and his troops were to land first as they would have the farthest to travel. They would be out of the LZ by the time the second wave of eight helicopters arrived carrying troops to go to the south tip of the peninsula. The units of the company command were to arrive ten minutes later and cover the east beach sector which was the primary landing zone.

The concept of the assault was to have the LZ cleared as rapidly as possible and have Bravo Company dug in before the arrival of the rest of the battalion. This was far from the ideal place in which to conduct a heliborn assault, but orders were orders.

The helicopters arrived on schedule and took on their human cargo. The assault was to land on the east beach coming from the north to the south. Looking out the open door of the H-34 all could see the LZ as they approached the landing site. The door gunner opened up with his machine gun spraying the vegetation beyond the river's narrow beach with machine gun fire. And then it happened!

For some reason known only to the pilot in command of the assault wave, they didn't land. They flew down in column to the point of the peninsula, the column reversed direction, and then they landed. They landed facing the river—not the beaches and the tree line—totally in the reverse order from that for which they had planned and in the way the troops were briefed. No good to worry about that now so they charged out of the choppers and up to the edge of the beach. There was momentary confusion and disorientation, but the careful briefing now paid off and Bravo Company began to function. The squads got organized, and David and his men were on the move. One of his fire team leaders started to dig in his fire team when a squad leader ran over to the man, kicked him squarely in the butt, and then asked the man: "Which way is the sun supposed to be when you face the river?"

The squad leader didn't have to wait for an answer. The man looked at the sun, then yelled at his fire team to get their ass in gear and move out. Plain, simple directions sometimes do wonders. There were similar occurences as the ensuing waves of assault troops arrived. The Marines would get out of their choppers, look at the sun and move to their assigned positions.

The terrain to the south was thick so David's advance was much slower than had been anticipated. His men had to chop their way with machetes for their was no beach on the south or west edge of the peninsula. There was only dense almost impenetrable jungle ten to twenty feet high laced with wicked thorns and razor sharp scrub trees. David wasn't yet in position, but the LZ was secure and the rest of the company was busy establishing a tight defensive perimeter. There sure as hell wouldn't be any VC of any strength down in the stuff David was trying to advance through, so Captain Wirsching radioed the Battalion HQ to bring in the remainder of the battalion.

And come they did—in giant CH-53 helicopters, 40 men at a time. There was confusion amongst the other companies as they set down. Troops milled about aimlessly, but eventually they got organized and began to exit the LZ area. For a while it looked like a miniature of the beaches at Normandy with so many troops jammed into that small area.

There had been one hell of a contrast between Bravo Company's landing and that of the rest of the battalion. Bravo's assault had gone very smoothly. It was not until late in the afternoon after David's platoon had cut a trail to the west edge of the peninsula that it became established in its position. The jungle was tough. By evening the entire battalion had arrived and was in place.

If the VC witnessed this circus they must have wondered what was going on. Here was an entire battalion on a small peninsula surrounded by a river—doing what? And in a very poor tactical position. A great many men in the battalion wondered the same. As it turned out the men of Bravo Company could be thankful that the enemy did not exploit their vulnerability. The new troops were learning to live in the jungle, to learn of the night noises, the total darkness, and the interdependence upon themselves and their buddies for survival.

They set up their night defensive positions interconnecting the fields of fire using vines for alert lines between adjacent fighting positions—procedures mandated by common sense. David's platoon could have been combat engineers for the amount of dirt they shoveled and the trails they cut.

The next day saw clearing skies and warm tropical weather. A resupply helo landed in the LZ and brought in Bravo Company's attachments and equipment of four rubber boats and two scout dog teams. Since Captain Wirsching had had previous rubber boat experience in recon, his Bravo Company was assigned the amphibious search and destroy mission along the banks of the river. They used the rubber boats to ferry one of David's squads across the river to provide security for the boats. On the peninsula side of the river they set up machine gun positions to provide fire support should the troops in the boats come under fire. Meanwhile another platoon swept the peninsula side riverbank prior to the arrival of the boats.

The resulting show was as though Disneyland were transported to this remote river in Vietnam with some added attractions. The rubber boats were hard to maneuver in the swift river currents and the inexperienced crews were often going around in circles. The two lead boats had the dogs who were supposed to smell the edge of the riverbank cliffs and smell out the hidden caves. All of this may have seemed feasible to the authors of the op-order, but the dogs wanted no part of this rubber boat business. All they did was howl like coyotes. The boat leading the armada had a Marine continually blasting the overhanging foliage with a shotgun to prevent any possible VC from throwing grenades into the water at the boats with the two scuba divers. All the fleet needed was a set of signal flags and a ship's whistle to be complete.

As the day progressed the boat crews became reasonably proficient and, blessedly, the damn dogs shut up. Nothing was found and the whole operation was becoming comical. Even so the troops were unrelenting in their search, never moving to a new section of the river until the supporting troops on the river banks were in position. While not very fruitful otherwise, it was a good exercise in troop handling and coordination between platoons. Bravo Company was flexing its muscle.

That night was uneventful execept that they were invaded by horrendous river leeches which dwelled in the underbrush. Every man was covered by morning so they all stripped down naked and inspected each other to ensure that none of those insidious little bastards remained. All hands looked forward to leaving this hostile and wretched environment.

There was always the possibility that some sharp VC commander might see a golden opportunity and bring in some heavy weapons to really clobber the Marines as they remained exposed near the tiny LZ. Apparently the Battalion CO finally sensed this, for later that day he called for air evacuation back to Camp Evans. He must have realized the futility of the operation. All that was found was five bags of NVA rice and three boats. The rice was helilifted out and the boats were destroyed. The rice was USAID which the United States had given the Vietnamese and had probably been sold on the black market to the VC.

The battalion debarked from the helos on the road near Camp Evans and marched the few miles back to the camp where they were met at the entrance gate by the Regimental CO who ordered a company personnel inspection the next morning at 0800. The order was delivered by the regimental sergeant major, and 1st Sergeant McKinney was almost court-martialed for remarking to him: "You've got to be shitting me Whose crazy assed idea is this?" Later that evening a four

foot brown cobra was found in the Regimental CO's hootch.
There was no inspection the next day, ha, ha!

Despite the attempted harrassment, they enjoyed a fabulous dinner provided by the base support personnel for the grunt Marines. They even had ice cream and cold beer.

All of this was a welcome rest from the jungle. Soon they would return again to that brooding menace, but that night the Marines celebrated their heritage.

Camp Evans was quiet except for the nightly booming of artillery firing H&I rounds into the vacant countryside. And the old man had bitched about Bravo Company using 18 rounds to remove a troublesome and potentially lethal sniper. One could be pardoned for questioning the priorities in this mixed up God-forsaken war. The troops took it easy for a few days and caught up on much needed sleep.

# ELEVEN

Word was soon out that the battalion would conduct a-
nother heliborn assault with Bravo Company again leading the way. Presumably that duty rotated. Bravo was the
junior company so perhaps it was felt it needed the practice.
Rocky alerted the platoon commanders and they resumed preparations.

The mission was to land in the foothills of the mountains
about 40 miles southwest of Phu Bai near the village of Phu
Loc and then climb into the mountains to attack an NVA battalion reportedly encamped there—just where wasn't known.
The operation was expected to last at least four or five days.
The battalion would be leaving Camp Evans for good and was
told to pack up all its gear and load out by convoy on November 17 for Phu Bai.

The truck convoy to Phu Bai was without incident except
for one well remembered event. As it was slowly passing
through the streets of the city of Hue a young blond-haired
French girl drove past the convoy in a small sports car. Captain Wirsching lost complete control of the company. She
was propositioned by every Marine on the trucks as she
slowly drove past. She was the first round-eyed, white
girl that the troops had seen in months. Captain Wirsching
turned helplessly to his first sergeant who smiled and said:
"Let the troops have their fun." In truth, the young girl enjoyed the exchange also.

Early the following morning the troops were assembled
for a final inspection. They were ready. One last change
was made. Captain Wirsching was informed that he was to
take a group of combat photographers from the news media
with him. Just what he needed! He told them that if they

wanted to go they would have to go in the first wave or not at all. He was surprised when one gutsy man from NBC said he wanted to go, so the captain put him and his two helpers in the second chopper. Rocky was in the first chopper accompanied by his Battalion radio operator, artillery FO, and forward air observer. David was in the third chopper with his CP and two machine gunners. The rest of his platoon followed in the next five choppers to secure the landing zone.

Five minutes until touchdown. Through the open doors the jets could be seen diving upon the objective area as they unleashed their bombs and napalm onto the hills and crests overlooking the landing zone. The VC could have no doubt now about who was going where. Rocky gave the alert signal, an essentially meaningless gesture for everyone knew they were almost there. Then it happened again!

The choppers didn't land at the LZ, but flew straight toward the mountainside, swerved slightly and then set down at least half a mile beyond the agreed upon LZ. Did someone know something the men who were about to be committed to action didn't know? If so, it was too late for explanations now, but this definitely wasn't the landing zone.

The photographers got some excellent pictures of David and his men as they jumped out of the chopper into the rice paddy and splashed toward the cover to the tree line. One of them, sporting a magnificent red beard and tiger stripe utilities, stayed with Bravo Company throughout the operation.

David and his men secured the area after which the remainder of the battalion landed at random locations and in various degrees of disorder. There was no incoming fire so the battalion gathered itself together and passed through first platoon's lines into the surrounding hills.

The assault schedule called for Bravo Company's lead elements to be at the top of the first hill by noon, an impossible task. Apparently the regimental operations planners didn't realize that when those little brown contour lines on the map got very close together, it meant that the climbing was almost straight up. The slope of the hillside was at least 60 degrees and densely vegetated.

Out came the machetes and up they went, ever so slowly. They went up in two parallel, mutually supporting columns about a hundred meters apart. The going was necessarily noisy, but surprisingly little noise carried through the dense jungle. There were no trails; they wouldn't have gone on them anyway. By nightfall they gained the summit of the first crest; even so, some of the men had to tie themselves into trees so as not to roll downhill before they could get any sleep. It was still a long way up the mountainside.

The night was spent in the relative security of their isolation. They set out only light defenses as there was no way they could have been attacked in force because of the density of the surrounding jungle. The monkeys chattering in the treetops were disconcerting at first, but soon the troops learned to relax and get some sleep. Future nights would be far more dangerous.

The next morning they continued their advance. The terrain was much less hilly now and the going was easier. Delta Company found a trail and followed it toward the top of the mountain. They paid dearly for following the easy going when they were promptly ambushed and had about a dozen men wounded, several seriously. The men of Bravo Company could hear the fighting in the jungle away to their left front—carbines, AK-47's and grenades on one side and M-16's and machine guns on the other. Apparently the VC didn't even know that Bravo Company existed, and its commander planned to keep it that way. He wanted to be the ambusher, not the ambushee.

Along with the gentler terrain the vegetation thinned and the speed of their advance increased, but they still maintained two mutually supporting columns about 100 meters apart. The enemy was apparently in the area now so all faculties were alert for any sign out of the ordinary.

By nightfall the battalion was high on the mountainside and Bravo Company could only guess as to its own location or its tactical relationship with the remainder of the battalion. An altimeter would have been more useful in determining their location than a compass. Captain Wirsching conferred with the Cowboy and they came up with an approximate location. To refine their position he climbed a tall tree to look for bearings while David's platoon provided security. Rocky called down bearings and the Cowboy was able to plot them on a map giving them their approximate location. This would be useful should the Cowboy have to call in artillery fire.

They spent another uneventful night in the jungle with the chattering of monkeys and other night noises more familiar now. In the morning Captain Wirsching asked for and received permission to conduct a combat patrol in his company's sector of operations. Patrols were his specialty. He grew up in the farm country of Indiana, while David was raised in the mountains of the Southwest. Between them they concocted a non-standard but deadly combat unit using David's platoon and attachments. Rocky told the other platoons that they would each get their chance on the following days. David was the experienced platoon commander and they all understood why his platoon was selected for the first patrol. The company XO and the other platoons were to remain secure and undetected in their company base camp area. One platoon was to be on alert, ready to move out should immediate reinforcements be needed. The other was to stand down and take it easy as they would be on patrol the following day.

An infantry platoon normally has three squads consisting then of 14 men in each. This provided three maneuvering elements. An infantry battalion has four rifle companies, therefore four maneuver elements. For the purpose of the patrol at hand they formed four squads of 14 men each plus an extra M-79 grenadier, a machine gunner, his assistant gunner, and an ammo humper. Captain Wirsching took his artillery FO, the forward air observer, his fireteam of runners, and battalion radio operator in his command group. Two squads were under his direction, two under David's. With this arrangement they were ready to go gook hunting. They left their noisy flak jackets and all non-combat equipment such as packs in the base camp. Their faces were painted out green. Rocky inspected every man for noise when he moved, verified the ammo count, the operational efficiency of the radios, and then they moved out.

Not for nothing had David been commended and became a member of "The Order of the Snake" while at Oklahoma Military Academy for crawling 400 yards through the grass on his belly while on patrol and getting to within 20 yards of the enemy patrol undetected. Now he and his platoon sergeant had the men well practiced in the art of silent movement. There were almost 80 men in this combat patrol and they made the noise of but a few.

Soon the point found signs of recent movement. About ten minutes later the lead scouts confirmed that there was a small group of about 20 or more VC not far away. Rocky sent a runner to fetch David and they held a conference. The terrain between them and the VC was relatively open as are the woods of Virginia in the fall. Surprise would be hard to achieve across the hilltop and an assault would have left them too long exposed before they could get to within effective range. Still, the patrol was undetected so there was a good possibility of capturing them all. Live prisoners with information would be extremely valuable. They formed a plan.

The VC were on the open crest of the hill. Just to the south of them the mountainside dropped steeply downwards. If they went down the mountain and advanced parallel to the crest along the almost vertical hillside, they could move undetected to within a few yards of the VC before they attacked. David took one squad to within 100 meters of the VC and very carefully set them into position. Their job was to protect Rocky's two squads should they be discovered and to prevent the VC from throwing grenades down the hillside at them. David's other squad was in immediate reserve in case of a screwup.

Slowly and carefully Rocky led his two squads down and then across the mountainside. Then they all got in line and very slowly, with great deliberate care, each man inched his way toward the summit. They were about 70 meters below the crest when they started and it required more than an hour to crawl within 10 feet of the crest, still undetected. They could hear the VC talking in their childlike, high pitched voices as well as the crackle of their radio as they sent out and relayed radio messages. Rocky signaled his radioman, who was farther down the hill behind him, to call battalion for permission to attack. He radioed the message, received a reply, then gave Rocky the thumbs down signal. Rocky couldn't believe that he had seen correctly. Here they had the tables turned on the enemy and the god-damn battalion had to get some village chief's permission to attack. They waited, but still no permission. After about a half-hour of this strain someone made a noise and the VC scurried down the opposite side of the hill. Rocky radioed to David to hold his fire as they were coming over the top. There was a lot of whooping and hollering as Rocky gave the signal for assault over the crest of the hill, but to no avail. The enemy was gone. The Cowboy, quick thinking bastard that he was, ordered an artillery barrage laid down in the direction of the VC's travel. Rocky radioed the battalion to inform them he planned to pursue the enemy. The reply was: "Stand in place," soon followed by the order to return to their base camp.

The march back to the base camp was very tactical because the VC now knew that Bravo Company was in the area and was a force to be respected. They dropped off a delay ambush to pick off any VC who might follow, but saw no sign

of the enemy. That night, unlike the night before, was an anxious one with every sound questioned. The party was over.

With the coming of daybreak Bravo Company was ordered
to a new location, but still had no new mission. The other
troops had heard of the assault on the hill and were itching
for their turn. Bravo Company was now the equivalent of a
200 man recon company—grunts who moved through the jungle,
left not a trace, and made no sound—a ghost-like force that
could raise havoc with the enemy were they permitted to do
so. Rocky didn't know the finer points of commanding an infantry company, but he did know how to patrol and David was
equally adept at leading where cunning and stealth would win
the day. Bravo Company was now something neat, something
special. The troops were no longer just ordinary grunts and
they were proud of it. As yet they had sustained no combat
casualties, but too soon that would change.

From the positions plotted on Bravo Company's map it
became apparent that the entire battalion was starting to retreat from the mountain. Bravo Company was the farthest up
the mountain and informed the Battalion CO that its condition
would rapidly worsen if it were not soon resupplied. He got
the message. At 10:00 PM three H-34 helicopters arrived.
There was no LZ so the company directed the choppers to their
position by throwing illumination grenades into a bomb crater,
then the air FO talked them forward.

That morning Bravo Company received orders to move off
the mountain and march down to the highway by the sea. It
was a very long way to travel. Much to the company's dis-
comfiture the Battalion XO appeared on the scene. He started
barking orders which only confused the platoon leaders and
undermined the usual well ordered sequence of preparation
and movement. Captain Wirsching sent his runners to summon
the platoon leaders so that he could detail to them a plan of
movement. The runner to the 3d platoon returned and informed
him that the Battalion XO had taken off with the 3d platoon.

The 3d platoon commander was a new 2d lieutenant and
had been intimidated by the major; furthermore, he neglected
to tell Captain Wirsching that he was leaving. Soon the company radio barked; it was the major ordering Bravo Company
to move out immediately and catch up to him. Rocky was mad.
This idiot might be a major and the battalion XO, but he was a
jerk. There he was strutting on down the mountainside, still
six or seven miles from the base of the mountain, with Bravo's
3d platoon as fast as he could move with no regard for security

or the comfort of artillery support. Rocky hoped that if the platoon got ambushed the VC wouldn't miss so inviting a target as his big ass.

When three platoons move they usually assume the shape of a triangle. "Two up and one back," is the old cliche. They are all thus mutually supporting. When two platoons move there is always a blind side, especially if they have to progress single file in column. The VC could well spot this weakness; they weren't dumb.

Second platoon took the lead flanked on each side by fire teams 50 meters away. These would help in breaking up an ambush, but not nearly as effectively so as two platoons in parallel routes of advance 100 meters apart. The company XO was at the point alert for trouble or an ambush from the front. Rocky was behind the second platoon with his command group. David's platoon brought up the rear and had rear security. This was not a good order of movement, but it was the only possible one under the circumstances. The rest of the battalion was either off the mountain or near the foothills and rice paddies. The two platoons of Bravo Company were still high in the mountains—the farthest away during the advance and the last ones given the order to leave, and now it was hurry, hurry, hurry.

They had been traveling only a few minutes when the major started to bitch over the radio for the rest of the company to catch up. Rocky solved that problem by putting one of his very slow talking black radio operators on the radio to talk to the XO. That private's deep southern cajun drawl was almost unintelligible so finally the XO abandoned his harassment by radio. The trail was very narrow so the movement was slow.

Suddenly, violently, the silence of the jungle was shattered by the sharp reports of rifle fire to the rear. Bravo Company's rear elements were under attack. Normally David's platoon had point, but today it covered the more vulnerable departure. In a few minutes all was silent, and the only word on the radio was enemy contact to the rear. The 2d platoon circled the wagons and awaited Rocky's command to move out back and help David. The company XO had the situation well in hand at the front. He was an experienced 1st lieutenant who knew his job well.

To the rear the enemy had sneaked up behind 1st platoon and opened fire. One man fell immediately and another was hit. David saw a Chinese grenade roll by as he directed a squad to come up on the flank, but it never went off. One of the machine gunners snatched up his weapon, dashed upon the trail, and stood over the corpsman and the dying man like a young lion, firing from the hip. Then the wounded man came back by David clutching his shoulder with a look of unbelief on his face. Now David turned to his radio man and snatched the hand set from him because he was frozen into inaction, round eyed and as pale as a sheet. The engagement didn't last five minutes, but it seemed an eternity before they were able to recover their fallen comrade's body.

It was the first time that David had watched anyone he knew die. The new lieutenant had survived his baptism of fire, conducting himself as an officer is expected to. After that when he came around the men, especially the veterans, they stiffened a little straighter and said "sir" with a little more deference.

Rocky knew better than to bother David on the radio until he was able to call. Presently the company radio came to life. It was David. He was panting as he delivered a brief coded message. Rocky asked him to repeat it, but he knew all too well what it meant. David quickly signed off and said he would get back as quickly as possible. Rocky was glad his cajun was on the battalion radio as the people there kept calling with all sorts of useless demands for information. He didn't need that bullshit then; he was busy and thinking.

Rocky informed Battalion HQ that they had made enemy contact, that was all he knew—end of message. The Cowboy had artillery standing by. The air FO had a pair of Huey gunships enroute. What wonderful troops! No one had to tell them what was needed; they knew and responded on their own.

Now Rocky informed the 2d platoon commander, his XO and his command group of David's message; 1st platoon had had a man killed. The bubble had burst. To the many new troops in the company it was still a shock to truly realize that death was so close at hand. There was profound silence for a moment, then the officers and NCO's responded with a nod and returned to their positions.

Presently David called again. The dead man was Willie Broadnax, a black from Jackson, North Carolina. He had seen the ambush and heroically jumped toward it firing his rifle. He was shot in the upper back and died rapidly despite the valiant efforts of the hospital corpsman who was immediately at his side. The men of 1st platoon charged after the enemy, but they vanished into the underbrush. Now they prepared to carry their dead comrade out from the jungle.

Rocky finally answered Battalion and informed them in a

few coded words of the status of Bravo Company. He handed
the handset to the radio operator and informed him to "get the
message through" relating to the administrative details of a
man killed in combat. Rocky's cajun now suddenly spoke
the King's English fluently. Rocky proceeded to the rear of
the column to meet David, who had his platoon reformed and
was headed to the front to meet the captain. They feared a
possible return ambush from the rear so it was agreed that
David would move out his platoon with two squads back and
one forward in the middle. The center unit carried Willie's
body up to the 2d platoon's position. He was carried on a
pole on a stretcher sling, for he was a big man of some 230
pounds. Second platoon traveled with two squads forward
and one behind, and with extra flank security.

The going was slow and deliberate. The squads and platoons were all now mutually supporting with their only objective to get down off the mountain. Under this circumstance
further ambush was possible but not likely. The gunships
on station had to refuel, but promised they would return later.
The artillery, however, was still standing by. The trail was
narrow and had to be widened at points to permit passage of
their buddy's body.

The two lead squads flanked each side of the trail by 50
meters, with the squads rotating the duty between platoons.
At one time or another every man in the company helped to
carry their comrade's body down from the hill. The terrain
was tough, but the Marines charged through the underbrush
with reckless abandon just daring the VC to stand and fight.

Ever so slowly they descended the mountain. Far in the
distance the 3d platoon could be seen entering the expanse
of rice paddies below, marching toward the coastal highway.

The sun was sinking in the west, but the trail was still
as unyielding as ever and there was the constant necessity
of hacking it wide enough for the polebearers to pass. As
they approached the base of the foothills and entered the
rice paddies the two lead squads fanned out in wide disper-
sion. The water was deep so Willie's body had to be floated
on an air mattress as the mud was too soft for his bearers to
walk weighted down as they were by their burden.

Darkness was all too fast approaching. The 3d platoon
radioed that they were encamped in a schoolyard near the
highway in the village of Phu Loc, a habitation of about 3000
people. The company interpreter confided that this was a
bad village, mostly VC by night. Just great! If the battalion

staff was aware of the hostility of this habitation it had never informed Bravo Company. Rocky signaled for the company to reform single file in a column of march as the lead elements of 2d platoon entered the village.

Bravo Company had no map of the city so the only alternative was to close up the column and keep moving eastward toward highway one and the sea beyond. And then it happened! In the blackness of the night and unfamiliarity with the surroundings of this strange location, the two front squads of the column got lost and were separated from the rest of the company. What an ideal setup for an intramural firefight.

Rocky called for the Cowboy and told him to get illumination right now. For a few minutes the VC had an opportunity to ambush Bravo Company but good. Evidently they were astonished by being invaded from the mountains at dusk by an infantry company. Five minutes later the sky overhead began to light up as on the fourth of July as the air FO scrambled a flareship from Danang airstrip. With this brightness the lost elements of 2d platoon soon returned to the fold, whereupon the company formed up tactically and swept on line through the village toward the sea. The combat sweep of the village hadn't been planned for, but if any VC were in town that night not a one was in sight. While it was an impromptu assault it worked and the troops arrived at the highway intact still carrying their fallen comrade. Rocky instructed the FO's to shut off the sky lights and to relay a very much appreciated "well done" to the artillery batteries and to the air wing.

At last they joined with the wayward 3d platoon. Captain Wirsching was not at all sociable and had little to say to the Battalion XO, but the atmosphere fairly crackled with bitterness and resentment. The Company XO and lieutenants set in the company for the rest of the night as a truck arrived to take their fallen Marine from them. Here and there was a silent tear as he began the long journey back to his home.

It had been a sad, sobering day, but Bravo Company was functioning. It had been bloodied, but would soon put the shoe on the other foot.

Early the following morning Bravo Company was assigned the task of guarding a detachment of Navy Seabees who were building a bridge and maintaining a section of the infamous "highway one." The bridge was located near Phu Loc halfway between Danang and Phu Bai. Phu Loc would later be completely wiped out by the NVA-VC at the beginning of TET and not retaken until February 1968.

The battalion staff became a semi-detached unit consisting of the major and a few men. He was to be in overall command of two rifle companies, Bravo Company and another one which was assigned similar guard duty about ten miles farther up the road. This miniature battalion staff was to prove worse than useless. It had far too few capabilities to be of any support to the infantry companies and just enough horsepower and BS to eternally screw up details. In fairness it should be added that this ineffectiveness was not characteristic of the Marine Corps.

The commander of the Seabee unit was a knowledgeable Navy lieutenant who gave Bravo Company the low down on what was needed. He was extremely glad that the Marines had arrived. The Seabees, were repairing the highway and rebuilding a vital bridge there. The people in the last unit assigned to guard the bridge had been lazy; consequently, the VC had blown up the bridge the first night they stood guard. Captain Wirsching informed the Navy lieutenant that he would send his best platoon to guard the bridge. David got the job.

The bridge was a beehive of activity. David had a squad continually patrolling each side of the approaches to the bridge, and from its span could be heard the periodic "whomp" of hand grenades as they exploded in the river below. About three that morning, the notorious major called down on the radio to complain about the noise David's men were making. Apparently his staff couldn't sleep. The company radioman deliberately ignored the protest. Rocky never knew where David got the cases of grenades, and he knew better than to ask. But in the morning the bridge was still intact. David turned the bridge duty over to another platoon and then proudly his troops marched into the Seabee camp. The Navy knew they were in good hands.

That afternoon the men of David's platoon went down a squad at a time, to bathe and wash clothes at the bridge which was being secured by two squads of the 2d platoon. The river must have been a sewer for half of Vietnam; what's more, it was filled with barbed wire and dud grenades. But for an hour while they washed and swam it was their paradise.

Beyond the element of duty, he and the other men of Bravo Company had reason to be grateful for the treatment they received at the hands of the Seabees. Here they learned the real meaning of the phrase "to take pity on." When

112

they arrived they were a sorry lot—drenched, blistered, sore, hungry, tired, and without good water. The Seabees took pity on them. They fed them hot chow and used their back-hoe to help them scoop out "hootches" (shelters) in the hill-side to finally get out of the rain. After that David declared: "If I ever get in some kind of march where I have to carry a sign, it's going to say, 'The U.S. Navy has pity'."

The rest of the company was assigned duty elsewhere and David's platoon was all that was left to guard the Seabees and a six gun battery of artillery that had also moved in. The bat-tery commander had begged Captain Wirsching for a profes-sional infantryman to set up the defenses. They could hear fighting from time to time in the hills around them so they knew the enemy was in the area, and the artillerymen were very edgy because they knew that the VC received special rewards if they destroyed a 105 with a satchel charge.

David, very cocky, said, "Sure, don't sweat it," and set out to defend a half mile perimeter with an understrength platoon, 12 men who could be spared from the battery, and a few new-comers who had arrived on a convoy from Phu Bai. When he was done the line was stretched out super thin, but he was confident that he'd made good dispositions and almost hoped the VC would come up.

The Seabee camp and the artillery battery were located about two miles south of the village of Phu Loc, the same place where Bravo Company had conducted its random night sweep a few days earlier. As stated, it was a beehive of VC activity. The battalion mini-staff in its infinite stupid-ity now added spicing to the cake. First it directed that a platoon be continuously on patrol in the foothills of the moun-tains, as well as maintaining an observation post on the hill-top which overlooked their position and the surrounding valley. In theory this plan may have seemed realistic, but in practice it was futile. First, the VC wouldn't move into or out of Phu Loc in the daytime so the observation post was useless. Sec-ond, the VC were entirely familiar with the countryside and could easily evade the wandering foot patrol. The artillery battery, by the necessity of geography, was exposed below and towards the mountainside to the south outside the organic perimeter of the camp (which by now was known as Camp Broadnax in honor of the Marine they had lost a few days earlier). All of this meant that the company was badly ex-tended protecting all of the elements committed to it for safeguarding.

But Captain Wirsching had an ace in the hole. Attached to Bravo Company was a soldier whose kind was code named "Kit Carson Scouts" by the Marine Corps. Bravo Company's was a real man who had been an NCO in the North Vietnamese Army and had switched his allegiance. He had been in their army for eight years fighting the South Vietnamese, but became disenchanted when the NVA wouldn't let him go home to see his girl friend up north. He was paid well by the Marine Corps. Captain Wirsching gave him the rank of sergeant and made sure that his troops respected him as such. He would have commanded respect in any army. He knew the jungle, the VC, the NVA—how they thought and would react. Many of the non-standard tactics and policies of Bravo Company were based upon his advice and recommendations. It was this "Cho Hoi," as he was known in Vietnamese, who had spotted the sniper on the hilltop during the first patrol southwest of Camp Evans. He was now again about to earn his keep many times over.

He was given sufficient funds for spending money and expenses, then told through a Marine interpreter to go into Phu Loc, have a good liberty, and ascertain where the VC were located and what they were up to. Their scout smiled and departed. Vietnam is an old country where bribery is a way of life, a fixed institution in the accomplishment of daily tasks and needs. A few days later the Cho Hoi returned.

Camp Broadnax was surrounded by low lying rice paddies which extended outward toward the foothills at the base of the mountains. Daily the farmers would leave the village of Phu Loc and come to tend their crops. Farmers? Hell no. There were a few who were particularly phony. Rocky spoke with David about this. They made no overt moves towards the fake farmers other than have a squad make a routine check of their identity cards. They did however, note the movements of the imitation farmers and learned that they were watching Camp Broadnax rather than tending their crops. Crops are tended in an orderly progression not random patterns across the fields. Both Rocky and David were familiar with farm practices, and these guys weren't farmers.

Bravo Company's forces were hopelessly scattered, so now it was time to play poker. It was imperative that the VC not figure out their game. Rocky got with the Navy lieutenant and informed him plain and simple that they would probably be hit hard in a few days.

114

But the Navy had a secret weapon; the backhoe. It was now employed ceaselessly on the front lines of their perimeter with Marines joining in for finishing touches. By nightfall Camp Broadnax looked like a miniature Corregidor. The VC in the rice paddies must have gotten a real eyeful. Even with the Seabees Bravo Company didn't have nearly enough troops to man all of the fortified positions they had built. Rocky and David knew this, but hoped that the VC wouldn't. Meanwhile the Marines were busy training the Seabees to become grunts. With their own welfare in mind, they were most attentive to the instructions. They built a command bunker with a log reinforced roof on top of which was sandbagged in a menacing 50 caliber machinegun gratefully provided by the Navy. Camp Broadnax was rapidly becoming a formidable fortress.

The Choi Hoi scout returned after a good liberty with some female companionship, and brought back detailed information about the plans of the VC and NVA. They would attack the following night—Thanksgiving—probably in force. Now it was Bravo's turn.

The battalion mini-staff was encamped at the regional ARVN headquarters which was less than a mile from Phu Loc. If the major—the Battalion XO—visited Camp Broadnax, Rocky would have had to divulge his information, but as long as he remained away he was better off incommunicado in his bunker.

The Cho Hoi scout told Rocky that the VC planned to infiltrate a large force past Camp Broadnax so as to be on the seaward side of its positions. They planned to first take the bridge under fire. The remainder of the enemy—he didn't know how many, although he was certain that there were many NVA in the mountains—would attack the artillery which was the weakest position.

As the Seabees were now well fortified they would have to defend their own camp. There would be but one platoon at Camp Broadnax and it could not be tied down to fixed positions, but would have to remain uncommitted to permit a counterattack of the main enemy assault wherever it came.

The Battalion XO's order that a platoon be continuously on foot patrol in the area surrounding the camp was still in effect. If this platoon were called in to help meet the anticipated attack it would be both a violation of orders and an indication to the enemy that an assault was being expected. The plan was adopted to use this platoon as a barrier patrol to block the enemy's escape and keep them within the ambush killing zone that was being prepared for the VC. This would be a hairy task, and Rocky selected David's platoon to execute this perilous part of the plan. Marines don't usually move or attack at night, so the enemy would not be prepared for an assault from his rear. Camp Broadnax was their main target so it was probable that they would ignore the wandering foot patrol.

Only a few people in the camp knew of the impending VC attack. The fewer the better. Besides Captain Wirsching the only ones informed were the Navy lieutenant and his senior chief, as well as the lieutenants and their platoon sergeants. The artillery people were not told because their hurried preparations would give away the fact that they knew. The down card—the pair of aces—was that if the VC thought they were approaching an unsuspecting garrison, their approach to Camp Broadnax would be lackadaisical and haphazard.

It was Thanksgiving Day and the Navy came through for Bravo Company. A fantastic hot Thanksgiving dinner with all the trimmings came ashore for the troops.

The stage was set. About an hour before sunset Rocky radioed the squad manning the observation post on the hill to "ditty bop" back to camp. "Ditty Bop" was a company code word in their slang which meant to be obvious, to be sure that the enemy saw them leave the hill top. Had the mini-battalion staff radio watch been on the ball they would have heard the order, but they didn't so had no cause for alarm. Good!

After the OP squad returned from the hilltop the Navy had for them hot roast beef sandwiches, cold milk, and fresh fruit. Captain Wirsching briefed the squad leader and the ambush commander. The CO of this reinforced unit was a staff sergeant who was on his second tour in Vietnam. He was the platoon sergeant of the weapons platoon, a machine gunner by profession. The ambush unit under his command consisted of two complete machine gun sections, two extra M-79 grenadiers, the 81mm mortar FO, the Cowboy, and a full Marine infantry squad and squadleader. The VC and NVA would be infiltrating in the valley which was overlooked by the hilltop observation post. That is where they would bite the bullet!

After dark the hilltop squad, reinforced by the ambush unit, slipped silently through the eastern perimeter and returned to the hilltop. As the men neared the crest of the hill they crawled to the summit so as not to reveal themselves

116

against the skyline. When they were ready they relayed a
thumbs up message to the company CP by radio. All were
now ready waiting for Bravo Company to do its thing.

The night was very dark with the blackness haunting and
eerie. Ghostly images through the starlight scope revealed
the movements of the approaching enemy. The hilltop radioed
that the VC were walking carelessly in the open, single file
along a trail in the grass at the base of the valley. There
was not a Marine to be seen anywhere so the enemy had no
cause for alarm. Up on the hillside overlooking the NVA
column, perhaps no more than 400 meters away, the ambush
team was poised and ready.

At a given signal four tubes of 81mm mortars barked in
unison. The first four rounds were illumination; thereafter,
one tube fired continuous illumination while the other three
delivered high explosive, quick fuze. There was no letup
to the deafening roar. As the first illumination burst bril-
liantly, the squad on the hilltop commenced to fire. One machine gun set up a barrier of fire to the east of the enemy
preventing their escape, the other blocked the exit to the
west with a murderous screen of lead. The M-79 grenadiers
pumped round after round into both ends of the column. The
enemy was trapped. The infantry troops with their M-16
rifles concentrated their fusillade into the chaos that was
enveloping the VC and the NVA. A veritable hell of destruction rained down upon the enemy as the mortar gunners continued to release their deadly missiles as fast as they could
drop the rounds down the tubes. A two hundred square meter
area was completely devastated by the impacting explosives.
Over 200 rounds of 81mm high explosive mortar ammo was
expended. Bravo Company's surprise had been complete as
it shattered the silence of the night with its trump card.

Upon receipt of the radio message from the hilltop saying that all was in readiness, Rocky had dispatched a runner
to brief the artillery battery commander, but his men were
not similarly informed and were utterly astonished as the
terrible racket rent the stillness of the night. The surprise
was also complete at Camp Broadnax where at the first sound
of fire the Seabees came tumbling out of their tents, half
dressed, with weapons at the ready as they charged to their
preassigned defensive positions. Their appearance was comical as they sprinted in sheer terror for the defensive perimeter. The Navy lieutenant and his chief who had been
briefed about the coming show, headed slowly for the front

117

lines to calm their troops. There was no doubt about it now, the Navy was awake and alert.

A few minutes after the runner reached the artillery battery commander, the arty had the tubes of the big guns depressed to the horizontal while devastating beehive charges were loaded into the breeches. The plan was for the artillery to fire their beehive charges into the far hillside before the troops moved down from the hilltop. Soon they were ready to fire, but Rocky gave them a check fire until he got a report from the troops on the hill. But by now the Battalion XO was on the radio demanding to know what was going on. The noise he heard must have been earthshaking. Captain Wirsching informed him that they had ambushed a large reinforced enemy unit and were preparing to repel an expected assault on Camp Broadnax. He then requested permission to send his troops down from the OP on the hillside to charge into the ambush area and mop up. They reply was "negative," so there was now no need for the artillery to fire their beehive charges. Once again the battalion staff was screwing up the details. They had caught the enemy by surprise and had the upper hand; now they were denied permission to follow up their attack. The entire company from the CO on down was absolutely furious, but there was nothing they could do. Orders were orders.

It wasn't until daylight that the major gave permission for the hilltop squad to go down into the valley below. The carnage they found was horrible; all that was to be found were bits and pieces of flesh and clothing, battered equipment and a few weapons, but no bodies were located. The enemy was a tough breed, as tough as the Marines. They had returned in the darkness and carried away their dead and wounded. Officially Bravo Company could count no bodies so it received no credit. The results of the ambush were plain, however; the enemy had been badly mauled. The VC had been had and they knew it; they would not soon return. Had the hilltop troops been permitted to charge down into the carnage and mop up, the victory would have been complete. All felt they had been denied the fruits of their efforts. They had beat the VC at their own game; the Marines were now the toughest in the valley!

But the excitement of the night was not over for David. That morning, November 24, at 0330 he was out checking his lines to assure that security was tight prior to the ambush. The password that night was snake-bite. The men

of his platoon were, as usual, standing good watches. But
he found some new people from the rear area asleep, kicked
them awake, stood them all at attention with their weapons
in their hands, and swore to them and to himself that if they
weren't still standing at daybreak when he returned, he'd have
them shot.

A few holes later a snake bit him on the left index finger.
It was in a copse, pitch black, and he never saw or heard it.
It was probably a cobra, but he couldn't be sure. He knew
that one was supposed to catch the damn things, or at least
identify them, so the medical people would know what anti-
dote to give, but that was out of the question. His corpsman put on a tourniquet, but they agreed not to risk the possible complications of the cut and suck procedure electing,
instead, to try and get him to the hospital as quickly as possible. Despite the stringency of the circumstance, David remembered to leave instructions that the men he had stood at
attention be relieved at dawn.

The air FO, who was with him, immediately called for an
emergency medevac and scrambled a chopper inbound. But to
compound the situation the ambush occurred just about the
time the emergency medevac chopper arrived at the vicinity
of Camp Broadnax. The air FO told the chopper pilot what
was happening and requested him to continue toward the
camp, that all the firing was outgoing and friendly. But the
meddlesome Battalion XO now again stuck his nose into a
place where it didn't belong and ordered the chopper away.
The first medevac chopper ran low on fuel and had to return
to its base empty. It was 0630 before another chopper was
able to return and fly David to the hospital in Danang.

By then his hand was swollen like a boxing glove and
his arm was like a sausage up to the elbow. By that time
he was delirious, and, having vomited all the ham the CB's
had fed them that evening for Thanksgiving, was vomiting
bile. He got some 20 shots of anti-venum and what not.
When the physicians and surgeons ran out of places on his
shoulders and buttocks to stick needles, they started on
his thighs. He knew that, despite the pain and shots, he'd
get no purple heart. What he didn't know was that he would
get that later—for the ultimate sacrifice.

Within a few days he wasn't sick any more and the swelling had gone down, but his hand still throbbed. He was able
to get out of bed, approach the head worshipfully with his
soap and towel, and have the first hot shower since he'd

119

been in Vietnam.

Meanwhile, by daybreak of the morning of November 24 following the ambushing of the VC and David's snake bite, Bravo Company was reunited as a whole. David's platoon from the foothills as well as the ambush squad from the hilltop had returned. The Navy supplied the beer and all hands with the exception of the bridge detail were allowed to take their packs off and relax. But their vacation at Phu Loc was nearly over. Soon they would be going north to the DMZ, to Con Thien, to no man's land.

It was there that Rocky Wirsching saw his final action with Bravo Company. The summer before he went to Vietnam he had undergone knee surgery to correct damage sustained in a skiing accident. It had caused him increasing trouble throughout his stay in Vietnam. During the fighting he further damaged the knee while removing two machine guns from a downed chopper. The exertion of sprinting to the chopper while under fire and then removing the weapons from their mountings was too much for his damaged knee, and he was transferred to a desk job in the headquarters of MACV in Saigon, a paper work job at "Fort Fumble" as it was known to the Marines that were there. Most of their efforts were a total waste in contrast to the dedication and sacrifice of the Marines fighting in the DMZ. The Marines fought for every inch of the ground they gained, while all too often the staff officers of MACV spent their time chasing the whores of Saigon and playing slot machines in the officers clubs.

# TWELVE

Rocky Wirsching was replaced as commander of Bravo Company by Captain Robert E. Harris who, like David, was formerly an enlisted Marine who was commissioned and serving again in Vietnam. Shortly after this transfer of command, on December 7, David was discharged after two weeks at the hospital in Danang. He rejoined Bravo, but he and Rocky were never to meet again although they corresponded regularly until David's death.

Just before he left the hospital he met some new arrivals there from his platoon who had recently been wounded. Disabled as they were, they expressed enthusiasm to find out that he was returning and assured him that everyone would be glad to get him back: someone who knew how to run a platoon (and although he had certainly never coddled anyone) someone who was fair. David reported: "Naturally I glowed with self-satisfaction. I know how to do this job; I wouldn't have come back if I didn't."

The next day he traveled north to Dong Ha, and on December 9 rejoined Bravo Company at C-2. There artillery and rockets were a constant fact of life, with the incoming disrupting camp routine at any time. On one occasion church services were interrupted. David was going to throw the Chaplain into his fox hole, but the man of the cloth depended more on his own nimble feet than any Godly intervention and beat David to this haven of relative security.

In the weeks following David's return, Bravo Company had just enough killed and maimed to keep them alert. Extremely bad weather hampered field operations and made resupply of all units very difficult. Air transportation was grounded for much of the time and roads were nothing but seas of mud.

On Christmas day of 1967, despite the truce at the time, David was out on patrol just like any other day. He urged his parents not to believe any press release that all the troops in Vietnam had a hot Christmas meal. The season did, however, bring him good news of sorts. He believed that they would remain in a more or less static position at C-2 for at least the next month; furthermore, he and his men had been able to fix his CP bunker up halfway decent.

At that time Douglas was enrolled at the University of Indiana. By way of encouraging his brother, David wrote: "Hope you're making it OK. Patience, old man, and you'll get there OK. Take care, do a little hard work, and from time to time say to hell with it."

His own morale, as always remained high. Typical of his attitude, he wrote: "I love my work. It's frustrating as hell, but I love it."

It was remarkable that the same person who felt mentally tormented almost beyond endurance during his years of athletic competition and marriage could write home with casual serenity: "The stresses and strains over here don't bother me much, but things like my W-2 form do, so I'm sending you mine."

On January 16, 1968, he caught a convoy to Dong Ha to complete his physical for a regular commision. Interestingly enough, Dong Ha was less than eight miles from C-2, yet the road had to be swept for mines each time before a convoy ventured upon it.

As January neared an end the monsoon was over and the enemy started spring campaigns, so action was expected to pick up. The cease fire for the Vietnamese holiday of Tet was broken and the troops on both sides were again "at it tooth and nail." Contact with the opposition infantry continued to be desultory, but they took some real shellackings from their artillery. There had been some bad wounds but luckily no one had been killed yet.

Life at Camp C-2 continued the pattern of dodging incoming and routine patrols through January and well into February. One patrol on February 16 turned out to be not so routine. The 2d platoon of Bravo Company was sent out in helicopters to protect a chopper which had been shot down while extracting a recon patrol. When they got there they advanced on the downed chopper, but the NVA were already in it and opened fire killing and wounding several Marines. Second platoon was in turn surrounded and spent the rest of the night fighting off gooks. The NVA were so close to the beleaguered platoon that artillery and air support couldn't drive them off without the risk of hitting Americans.

The next morning at dawn the rest of Bravo Company, with David's 1st platoon leading the way, marched to help them. After about three miles they began to hear the firing about a half a mile off. In order to avoid an ambush but still make time toward the sound of the fighting, David had to pick terrain which required some heroic machete work. They circled around and cut their way through a jungle of thorn bushes. David got impatient with the progress and snatched a machete himself with which he began slashing at the thorns, gashing his hands in the process. When they got through they deployed along a tree line and fired in the direction of the AK's (Communist weapons with a different sound than American arms). They didn't see any of the enemy or of their own Marine comrades, but soon the firing stopped so they moved on into 2d platoon's perimeter. The battle scene as they came upon it was just like in the movies—the litter of the battlefield and the dead strewn around in picturesque attitudes.

Right off David saw two Marines caring for a third who had been wounded. The wounded man looked up with a vacant stare, but recognized David and said, "Lieutenant Westphall, water, water," so David gave him one of his canteens. Then Lieutenant Johnston, the CO of 2d platoon, came up, grabbed David by the hand and gratefully exclaimed: "I've never been so glad to see anyone in my life!" First platoon took over the most dangerous part of the perimeter, but the hidden enemy didn't fire again until the choppers came in for the wounded, and even then the discharge was only sporadic. The whole of Bravo Company peppered the bushes as each chopper came down, which was SOP. There was no answer from the enemy.

The people from Bravo Company found NVA battle dressings covered with blood. As they recovered the bodies of their fallen Marine comrades, they learned that the enemy had stripped them of their battle dressings, apparently to use them on their wounded. This grisly finding was an indication that the NVA must have sustained heavy causalties. As David examined the crashed chopper he recognized some of the recon bodies as from a squad that had passed through his camp several times. There was one Marine survivor who had spent the night lying wounded in the darkness surrounded by the enemy. David was assigned to question him and learned that, considering his experience, he still retained an amazing amount of the famous recon <u>sang-froid</u>.

After the wounded and dead were air-lifted away, David's platoon covered the rear as the company left the field, but there was no more action. None of his men were hurt in the operation. Later that day they came upon two companies from 2d battalion, 1st Marines out from Con Thien and spent the night with them in the field. By the following day the enemy had vanished from the area so the two groups returned to their respective camps.

By February 20, 1968, David had been in Vietnam long enough so that he could put in for R&R whenever the quotas came out, which he expected to be within a few months. The nostalgic thought of a rest and recreation period away from a forward area caused him to consider his future philosophically. He wrote confidingly to Douglas:

> My morale is pretty good, and, after all these years—all the adventures I've been through right here inside my own brain—I've finally reached a state in which I can manipulate my mental equilibrium so as to never be actively happy or unhappy, but instead, which is best, constantly pleasantly contented. I suppose I've become "philosophical." I'm my own worst enemy, and I approach knowing myself, so how can any one else hurt me?

David retained this philosophical calm to the very end of his life. He had no part of the bluster and swagger that men seem impelled to assume when they are alone among their kind, perhaps to bolster their own failing egos and prop up their faltering courage. Yet he meshed smoothly with the rank and file, both those whom he ordered and took orders from. He enjoyed the respect—according to some reports even adoration—of his men. At one time he overheard the artillery forward observer and forward air controller (sergeants who went out attached to the various platoons to help control their respective supporting arms) discussing their superior officers. They said they much preferred being with 1st platoon and felt safest with them because lieutenant Westphall was the only one around who really knew his business and could really read a map.

David concluded: "I don't know how my superiors think

I'm doing, but it's encouraging that the men whose lives are in my hands have trust in me. We're due for a contact soon and we'll see if I know my business."

Camp C-2 nominally required 8 platoons or more. Late in February they only had 5, and David speculated that if the gooks knew of this deficiency they might be tempted to attack. To make bad matters worse, they were unable to get any claymore mines, so were compelled to work out a system of homemade bombs using demolitions, duds, and whatever else they could scarf up. Their difficulty was in devising a reliable firing system. David optimistically concluded: "Once we get one rigged up though I'd be almost ready to take down our wire so the gooks would be more tempted to get up close and among all the goodies we've concocted."

Life at Camp C-2 continued into late February with the usual frustrations and foul-ups, but David continued to keep in there pitching and trying to do as professional a job as possible. One day during the last week of February, Dong Ha was hit by 400 rockets. Since Dong Ha was the supply base for C-2, Con Thien, Yankee Station and other outposts, their supply system suffered greatly. The chow, which had been pretty good, began to deteriorate and they had no beer for over a month.

David wrote that he wouldn't be sending a check during March as he was leaving all his money on the books for R&R which he hoped to get in Manila in April or May. From time to time he alluded expectantly to this R&R, but it was destined to be deferred until his rest was a permanent one in a grave with thousands of his comrades in the National Cemetery at Santa Fe, New Mexico.

But for the present life continued. On the first day of March Bravo company participated in an operation in which David's platoon ran patrols to protect the rear of the rest of the company which waited in ambush as a blocking force for two other companies which swept a ville where, hopefully, there would be some NVA. As was so often the case, the net came up empty. According to a prisoner captured by another battalion, David's platoon passed through a ville where a whole NVA battalion was hiding. If they were, David believed, they were certainly well hidden. For the enemy to be well hidden was, of course, the rule rather than the exception.

On March 9 David's platoon moved to Yankee Station which was an outpost about a quarter of mile southeast of

Con Thien. The gooks seldom shot at Yankee Station, probably because there was no equipment of much value there.
Right then even Con Thien was taking minimal incoming. Apparently the opposition had decided to concentrate on Dong Ha
which earlier had been something of an R&R center, but was
no more.

B-1-4 outposted Yankee Station throughout 1-4's stay at
Con Thien from early in March to June 1968. Yankee Station
was the reaction company for Con Thien in the event of over-
running by the NVA.

The day before their move to Yankee Station David's platoon got a few shots at some of the enemy and called in some
mortars on them, but didn't know if they got any. That was
the only action they'd had in weeks. Things were so slow
contactwise that David volunteered for an aerial observer
quota. Had he gotten the job he would have flown in a piper
cub type plane while making $160 a month extra and seeing
more of the country. Anyway, the general policy for Marine
officer billets in Nam was six months as a platoon commander and the rest of the tour in some kind of a staff or support
job. David was already well past the six months.

Contact continued light throughout March, but all the
moving they'd been doing kept David busy with administrative
details. Since he was finally settled into what for at least
a few weeks promised to be a permanent position, he was
policing up on loose ends and getting a routine of sorts going.
He had another new platoon sergeant whom he had to train,
and wrote to his parents: "In the old days it was the salty
old sergeants who broke in the new, green lieutenants, but
these days the old, competent professional soldier of a sergeant is a myth of the past."

In order to break the tedium of filling sand bags, David
periodically challenged other platoon commanders to sand
bag filling contests in which more work was done in an hour
than would normally have been done in a week. His platoon
didn't lose a contest and they drank a lot of beer at other
people's expense. One opponent fell behind 132 bags in an
hour.

Near the end of March he was uncharacteristically chewed out by his company CO and XO for an incident that had
accompanying humorous overtones. It seems there was an
order that no one was to go outside his bunker without wearing his helmet and flak jacket. Some of David's men were
playing football without these items. They were discovered

and fined $25 each (David paid all of the fines). His radio operator (later killed at his side) went to the company head-quarters to deliver the fine money. On this errand, of all things, he forgot to wear his helmet and flak jacket. Everyone thought it was uproariously funny that he was compelled to add another $25 to the amount of money he was delivering.

During the first three weeks of April David's platoon fired on the enemy three times, but couldn't seem to really get their teeth into them. At least they hadn't waxed Bravo either. One day during this period, taking advantage of the relative inactivity, he flew over the north in a helicopter and saw some of the trails in use up there. But with May approaching he conjectured that the gooks could be planning some festivities which might include his outfit.

David made 1st lieutenant the day before Easter, which he considered a step in the right direction. At this time he also signed the papers for a six months extension in Vietnam. By taking advantage of the inducement the services offered for such extensions, he'd get a 30 days paid leave in Spain in September, all travel paid, in addition to his regular 30 days annual leave. He thought it might be possible to visit home enroute, but wasn't sure yet. Naturally he was looking forward to the trip. He was also about ready for an R&R, but couldn't seem to get on the list. He hoped that he would be soon so he wouldn't be held in Nam because it was too close to September. He dreamed even further of another R&R some time after he returned from Spain, which would enable him to see a little more of the world.

*     *     *

These nostalgic passages of fancy were made in a letter to his parents dated April 22, 1968. He would be killed exactly one month later.

*     *     *

Consequent upon his promotion he went up the hill from Yankee Station to Con Thien to deliver the battalion commander the beer and cigars that were traditional after a promotion (having been lucky to have wangled some from the rear for that purpose). Strolling along with his sandbag of goodies over his shoulder and his helmet cocked to listen for the freight-train rush of incoming from the North, that's exactly

127

what he heard. He dropped his bag, sprinted for the nearest trench, and dived. For the third time since he'd been in Nam a round landed right where he'd been standing. When he got out of the trench he went to look for the precious beer. One can was PIA (punctured in action), one was DIA (dented in action), and the other 14 were MIA (missing in action). He wrote home with unperturbed nonchalance: "Everyone thought it was a fine joke. My spirits remain high."

In a letter home of May 9, David noted that it was then a year to the day since the gooks over ran Con Thien, but added that it wasn't likely to happen again as the defenses had been strengthened considerably since then. Still they might try if they wanted a place like Con Thien for the peace talks that were to open within a few days.

About then David's mother inquired about some fighting she had heard about at Con Thien. He added in the same letter that part of Bravo Company was in it, but not his platoon as it had been in the field the previous day. He especially remembered this because he and his men had narrowly missed falling into an ambush. The enemy suffered 72 killed in this action at the cost of 9 Marines, and very probably a projected NVA attack was disrupted. The climax of this affair was a tank-infantry charge so stirring that the next day six clerks and motor transport people, who normally had nothing but jibes for the "grunts," volunteered to go on a patrol with David's platoon.

In this same letter of May 9, David wrote to his parents: "I should go through my papers and refer to your recent letters and answer your questions, but they're not handy now and it's been so long since I've written that I'll just continue and get this in the mail tomorrow." Thirteen days later he would be dead. Since he knew where his papers were then, his parents could never understand why they were not returned to them after his death.

David wrote his last letter to his parents on Mother's day, so it was addressed especially to his mother. He wrote:

Mom,

This won't get to you until after Mother's Day (today), and it won't have any flowers or anything in it, but I'm writing to let you know I didn't forget. There are some pretty flowers growing in the countryside here and I could have pressed some and sent them if I'd thought of it

in time. Even the Marine Corps remembered Mother's
Day and we had a chance, last pay day, to fill out forms
for sending flowers by mail, but I missed the opportunity
because I was taking the pay roster back to Dong Ha.

Don't let me forget your birthday. I know it's the
15th, but again I've forgotten if it's June or July, although
I think it's June.

You're probably having pleasant weather there now.
It rained here today which cooled things off some, although the temperature still got up to a muggy 95° with
the hot months still to come. After a rain here the air
seems to be more clear and you get a good view of the
mountain ranges to the west of us, and from the observation posts on "the hill" you can see the ocean to the east.
There was a really beautiful gold, pink, and light blue
sunset over the mountains in Laos this evening.

I've got to start paying more attention to my correspondence and somehow get caught up on it. Every time
I sit down to write something seems to come up. I got
another great letter from Kim today. I'll quote the first
paragraph. "First of all congratulations on your promotion to 1st Lt. your promotion is really too fast. By pro-
moting speed of your rank you will soon take over me."

Dad will read this and I also send him greetings and
good wishes. The change to better weather may have
slowed down preparations of the final parts of the Catron
biography. At any rate, I'm sure both of you are busy as
usual.

Mom, I hope you had a good day today. Take care.

Love,

David

Three days later he wrote his final letter home—to his
brother, Douglas. It was a long somewhat rambling missive
as though he were stitching together an ultimate mosaic of
odds and ends. Portions follow:

On June 1, unless I'm held back as a witness for a
pending court martial, which is possible, I'll be on R&R
in Hong Kong. I wanted to go to Manila originally, but
I'd been getting even better reports on Hong Kong so put
in for that port instead. By 10 June I'll be back to the

old grind, and who knows what will happen to break that up until September when I'll go to Spain at government expense for the 30 days free leave I get for extending over here for six months.

If things go as scheduled, the 25th of this month I'll be the new XO, and possibly a month after that a company commander [this speaks mutely to David's ability since company commanders were almost always captains] . I didn't get the aerial observer job so I went to the Bn. CO and told him I wanted to continue as a plt. commander while waiting for another command ie XO or CO, rather than a staff billet. When the battalion gets enough officers so they can afford to let me transfer, if I'm not satisfied with my situation here I'll transfer to 3rd Force Recon. I talked to the bn CO when I was in Dong Ha last month as a pay officer and he says he'd like to have me. For right now, though, I'm still a rifle plt. commander.

Both ground action and incoming around here have been sporadic, just enough to keep things from getting boring. 1st plt. Bravo has been in three fire fights with three wounded and no killed in the last month.

Since the bombing halt, as nearly as I can tell, there's been a pickup in enemy activity, but this could be only because it's the season of the year for increased campaigning. What I have noticed is a great increase in U.S. air activity in our area. Obviously what is happening is that the same number of sorties as previously are being concentrated in a smaller area.

I agree that the peace talks will probably be a farce. Our attack into the A Shau valley seems to hold out hope that finally we've learned that all Communists understand is force and that we need to secure an advantage of some sort to bargain with, but it is probably too much to expect of bungling U.S. diplomacy and our incursion into that stronghold and it's timing are probably just a fortuitous accident that we won't follow up.

David concluded his letter with a postcript which conveyed his final literary legacy to his brother. He wrote:

Have you ever read any of Ayn Rand? If not and you get the time and inclination I recommend Atlas Shrugged, and Capitalism: the Unknown Ideal.

On May 19, 1968, Bravo Company was alerted for a sweep around the area of Con Thien, designed to keep the NVA off balance. The operation was to start at 1000 the following morning. The Company CO, Captain Robert E. Harris, held his briefing at 1700 on the 19th. He already had orders transferring him to Little Creek, Virginia, for duty there, but informed his officers and staff NCO's that he was staying with them for this operation so that he could observe the new CO in the field. At the briefing, Captain Harris was presented with a fine watch from Switzerland as a going away present.

At the same time Captain Harris asked the platoon leaders for their report on a charity drive that was then being held. One of them refused to canvas his men because, as he stated, he felt that they were doing enough for Vietnam just by being there. He was relieved of his command and transferred immediately. Three days later he would weep tears of bitter anguish because of this transfer.

On May 20, a platoon from D-1-4 arrived at Yankee Station to garrison it while Bravo Company was away at war. When Bravo moved out morale was high, and everything that could be required of the Marines was covered by their instructions. They did not lack for anything. They had their full quota of attachments: air, artillery, mortars—a full boat so to speak. The weather was hot with the roads dusty and the grass deep.

They moved out in column with platoons staggered, 2-CP-1-3. Their direction was eastward, angling off between C-2 and Gio Linh. The terrain here slopes away from Con Thien towards the Ben Hai River, which is the center line of the DMZ. Their first night's defensive perimeter was about 500 meters north of the spot where B-1-4 had rescued a recon team earlier.

The second day the sweep moved northward towards the DMZ and the river, then to the west paralleling them. Most of the movement was visible from the OP on Con Thien. The company formation was on line with flankers out on both flanks. They found plenty of signs of the enemy—old fighting holes, trenches, gun pits and such. But they sighted no troops. There was a lot of sweat and dry throats as they methodically moved out. Bravo's night defensive positions were the same as the first night with, again, no action.

May 22 dawned bright, sunny, and very hot. Bravo Company continued to move in a westerly direction along the DMZ. A few Marines remarked that Con Thien looked different from this location. They could see bunker apertures against the blue sky background. Their formation was the same as before, and their progress was good. The grass was about waist high.

During the late afternoon halt the Marines were informed by the Battalion CO that they were to return to Yankee Station after 0800 on May 23, entering from the northwest. This was the area where B-1-4 had rescued A-1-4 back in March so most of the men knew the area rather well. Captain Harris issued the night orders at this halt. They were to pass through an old experimental pig farm and set up defensive positions about 500 meters beyond. As they passed through the farm the stench was still there to urge them on. Now the last order issued, as well as contemplation of their night halt, may have distracted their undivided attention that tiny bit which can sometimes mean the difference between life and death— good holes were to be dug that night because B-52's were to strike to the north and no chances were to be taken.

The terrain here was rolling with successive swales and ridges. The waist high Kunie grass was interspersed with patches of heavy brush, and hedgerows divided off the countryside. As they moved beyond the farm David's 1st platoon occupied its customary position at the point, providing a security screen for the headquarters group. Presently one of the long low rises that characterized the locality crossed their line of march. Several of the point men had crossed over it when an L-shapped ambush was sprung.

Suddenly, ferociously, Bravo Company was hit with a devastating fusillade of machine guns, mortars and grenades. The yell of "tubing" mingled with the din of battle, and most of the Marines hit the ground. Captain Harris promptly issued the command to open fire and move up. The men of Bravo as quickly complied, but no enemy was to be seen. Corpsmen were called for. Air and artillery FO's radioed for support.

Captain Harris ordered assault fire and personally moved out toward the point. Now some 100 of the enemy appeared in assault formation moving in on 1st platoon's lead squad— the point. Heavy weapons fire was sweeping the company's front from the north side of Bravo's line. The officers and NCO's moved out quickly trying to form a firing line to stop the assault. It was obvious that they knew their jobs as

132

they exposed themselves in the line of duty, and the enemy concentrated its fire on them. Most of the 13 killed and 27 wounded were lost at this time. These included every officer, radioman and all but two staff non-com's. But for their timely and heroic action, Bravo Company would surely have sustained immensely more grievous losses.

Captain Harris had moved up to cover a wounded machine gunner while his teammate got the gun back into action. He was killed instantly, shot through the heart. David rushed forward to move up a squad in order to build up the firing line and stop the enemy assault. He was killed as he advanced, struck by machine gun fire along his left side. His radioman, Charles Kirkland was killed by his side with the same burst of fire as he loyally stayed with him to provide vital communication. David's men of 1st platoon had idolized him, now one of them proved his devotion to his leader by giving up his life trying to save him and the others of Bravo Company.

The enemy assault wavered when it didn't see the 2d platoon as it moved in on the 1st to cover it, but some half dozen actually entered Bravo Company's lines before being killed or driven back. The engagement had started at 1720, now at 1740 the firing stopped as quickly as it had started. The 2d platoon, the farthest from the point of contact, closed up and formed a perimeter into which the CP moved. The wounded were attended to and brought into this tight perimeter, while the dead were placed side by side at the company aid station.

The NVA left 22 dead on the field as well as many blood trails as they withdrew. They also left strewn on the field of battle eight machine guns, three 60mm and two 81mm mortars, and 28 rifles.

The 3d platoon sent a reinforced squad on a fast sweep in the direction of the rise to check on the men who had crossed over. All were alive, but wounded. They came in on their own power. Battalion was notified of Bravo's predicament and soon helicopters came in to fly out the wounded.

B-1-4 spent the night in a very tight perimeter. No one thought of sleep or thirst, only of their heavy losses. At dawn D-1-4 with a platoon of tanks came out and escorted Bravo Company back to Yankee Station. The dead went back on the tanks. Later, at Charlie Med CO at Dong Ha, 1st Sergeant Tom McKinney saw and talked to the wounded.

They were just great—not angry, bitter, or remorseful—just stunned at their heavy losses. Then 1st Sergeant McKinney identified each of the dead—not an easy task, but a necessary one.

Looking back, the men of Bravo Company were professional Marines, each and every one. They were not angry with the enemy, or anyone for that matter. They were just doing the job for which they had been trained, and doing it well. The leadership was of the best. Captain Harris was killen on the day that he would have landed in Okinawa going home, but he would not turn over command to a younger officer until he had personally observed him in the field. David was way past his R&R, but he did not complain.

The lieutenant who had rebelled against the relief fund drive came to 1st Sergeant McKinney several times with tears in his eyes asking: "God, why didn't I stay with them? I might have prevented some of it." He'd had the 3d platoon on the right side of the line and the platoon sergeant had taken over as platoon commander for the operation. He was killed that day.

*      *      *

The question may be asked: "Could the ambush have been prevented?" The answer is an extremely qualified: "Possibly."

The first part of the qualification is to remember that the enemy was clever and resourceful; furthermore, he was fighting on his own terrain at times and places of his own choosing. For the Marines to lay casualties upon the enemy under these conditions was an accomplishment; to avoid destruction themselves was an even greater one.

The ambush might have been prevented by helicopters constantly searching out the path of the patrol's advance. But then there would have been no confrontation, and wars cannot be fought without confrontation. The same is true had the patrol been led by a tank column. But then the enemy would simply have ultimately moved to locations where tanks could not follow, and the bloody task of rooting him out would still have fallen upon men on foot following other men on foot into regions of the enemy's choosing.

Yes, that precise ambush might have been prevented but another would inevitably have been waiting elsewhere. If man would prevent all ambushes he would do better to master the divisiveness of the spirit which has been the evil genius calling the shots for armed conflict throughout the ages. True, one side of an argument cannot bring amicable settlement alone, but as surely as the sun rises one side can and must make the start without which no solution is even remotely possible.

# EPILOGUE

Soon after David's funeral we had to decide what to do with the $30,000 left by his life insurance policies. My wife, Jeanne, thought of setting up some type of scholarship with the money, but I discouraged that plan as being too ordinary. When she later suggested the "Vietnam Veterans Peace and Brotherhood Chapel," I grabbed the idea like a dog worrying a bone.

A little later we contacted Ted Luna, a young Santa Fe architect who was already establishing a reputation for innovative planning. Subsequently we commissioned Ted to design the Chapel, explaining to him only that the structure should be such that no person entering it could leave with quite the same attitude toward peace and war. We also indicated to him that there should be an eternal flame and two inscriptions.

The first of these was from David's poem: "The Ultimate Curse:"

> Greed plowed cities desolate
> Lusts ran snorting thru the streets
> Pride reared up to desecrate
> Shrines, and there were no retreats.
> So man learned to shed the tears
> with which he measures out his years.

The second was from his essay: "The Prophets and Their Times."

> At the sight of the heavenly
> throne Ezekiel fell on his

136

face, but the voice of God
commanded, "son of man, stand
upon your feet and I will
speak with you." If we are to
stand on our feet in the
presence of God, what, then,
is one man that he should
debase the dignity of another?

On July 7, Ted brought us the preliminary architectural
drawings for the Chapel. I noted in my journal that I considered the structure they represented to be magnificent and
inspired—surely one of the most beautiful buildings in the
world.

Visualize the Chapel as completed. It stands on a hill
in Northern New Mexico overlooking the beautiful Moreno
Valley. The vast gull-like structure rises above the brow
of the hill to a height of nearly 50 feet and has graceful, inward curving walls sweeping down to each side of twin center
pinnacles. The west wall is slightly the higher and longer,
and is a quarter-circle arc of a 99 foot radius. Both walls
flow majestically down from their commanding height so that
the tip of each recedes into nothing as it is buried in the brow
of the hill. A third inward curving wall completes the structure, which encompasses a relatively petite interior compared
to the massive exterior. The roof line follows the downward
curve of the two main walls to normal room height at their
juncture with the third wall.

On this wall are photos, eight inches by ten inches in
size, of Vietnam Veterans who gave their lives to the war.
Looking down from the photos one sees four descending con-
centric rows of curved seats and, looking upward the ceiling
soaring to the top of a window twenty-eight feet high which
extends to the floor level of the lowest tier of seats. The inward curving walls on either side confine the space and gently
lead to the narrowing apex of the room. Here a dynamic,
sharper, outward curve of the left wall ends the space at the
window which is only a single foot in width. To the left of
the window, so as to leave an unobstructed view through the
opening, is a simple cross bearing an eternal flame.

All this while the furies of mental torment over our son's
death were fuming in my wife's mind. Early on the morning
of July 12, 1968, I was awakened by a commotion which I
found to be Jeanne frantically scurrying about the house pul-

ling all electrical plugs from their sockets. When I questioned her she frenziedly broke from my grasp to continue her search for more plugs, explaining hysterically that the house was about to blow up. I finally quieted her when she was assured that there were no more plugs to be disarmed. Her fear appeared to be genuine and frightening.

A curtain may well be drawn over the exact sequence of her travail. Suffice it to say that she was afraid to live any longer at Val Verde, so I took her to stay with her sister in Albuquerque. She remained there intermittently until we sold Val Verde on May 22, 1969, exactly one year after David's death. I then moved our belongings into a mobile home at Springer, New Mexico, sixty-five miles across a mountain range eastward from the Chapel. Here my wife joined me on September 7, but on March 3, 1970, she again felt uneasy even that far removed from the Chapel and returned to Albuquerque.

All this while the problems of my constructing the Chapel were unimaginably numerous and vexing. During these trying times, our surviving son, Douglas, was like a rock in his support of the Chapel enterprise, giving his aid in person whenever posssible and his undiluted moral support at all other times. My wife, also, lent her support within the limitations of her fears and long absences from the vicinity of our former home at Val Verde.

Early in March 1971, I moved our mobile home to Albuquerque, thinking that somehow I might be able to continue work on the Chapel from there. By May 22, the third anniversary of David's death, the Chapel construction was far enough along to permit a reasonably finished appearance for its dedication that day. Lieutenant John Kerry spoke at the dedication. An earlier address to a Congressional Committee in Washington had attracted national acclaim. The dedication was covered by all three television networks as well as the A.P., U.P.I., and N.E.A. wire services.

Following the ceremony I returned to Albuquerque, stopping on the way at the site in Springer from whence I had moved our modest home. The place was barren and stark, with the clothesline still standing. The free-standing vent pipe bore silent witness of a former habitation. But the grass of the newly planted lawn was green and needed attention. Songbirds were heralding the approach of summer. The atmosphere was serene and quiet. This tranquility was in marked contrast to the raucous din of the big city where I was headed.

As I stood in this pleasant setting, I realized the futility of trying to keep faith with David and the Chapel with a residence in far-removed Albuquerque. A few days later we moved our mobile home back to Springer.

When we reached there the grass was still green and the birds continued their joyous serenade. We were home again, and the monumental struggle to complete the Chapel and spread its message could continue.

What was that message? It can best be summed up by two newspaper articles presented to the public with an intervening time span of five years.

In the early summer of 1972 Gloria Emerson, of the New York Times, visited the Chapel and talked with me at length. She had just returned from two years in Vietnam. When she left she said: "Thank you for teaching me how to cry: I thought that I had forgotten how."

Subsequently she wrote an article which appeared in the June 15 issue of the New York Times, a portion of which said:

> The chapel is not just to honor the 13 men in Company B who were killed in Con Thien four years ago, or even to honor Americans alone.
> "There is some commotion today—of protest—when you say peace and brotherhood," Dr. Westphall said. "If I found out that the person who had killed my son... in turn had been killed, I would put his photo in the chapel."

Then Ms. Emerson added an important qualification:

> "I am not singling out the North Vietnamese, but I am not excluding them," he added.

On November 4, 1979, another article about the chapel, by Michael Satchell, appeared in Parade magazine. The article was headed" "One Man's Shrine To All Who Fell In Vietnam," then continued: "Without help from the government Marine's father builds chapel to honor the dead of both sides."

When asked about this point, I characteristically reply that it honors "all Vietnam veterans: the living, the dead, and the maimed in body and spirit." If pressed on the distinction of "all," I freely admit that my personal interpretation is just what I said, with no reservations as to race or nationality. But I just as quickly hasten to add that I will, without chagrin, allow each person equal latitude with my own.

It is the nature of human language that it is impossible
to encompass absolute meaning of a complex subject in a
single phrase, sentence, or perhaps even paragraph. Sometimes it is difficult to embrace full understanding in even an
extended presentation. This truism of human nature is difficult to understand for persons who see everything as either
all black or all white.

While I personally would have stressed different themes,
I found nothing the least bit offensive to my own sensibili-
ties in Michael Satchell's article. For those who did, let me
state what I would have stressed. First, and foremost, the
Vietnam Veterans Peace and Brotherhood Chapel is, as its
name implies, a monument to peace—not a war memorial. On
this point I am adamant. If full implementation of the concept
of peace demands the Christian attitude of extending the hand
of fellowship to former enemies, I will not demure. This
whole matter of friends and enemies is, after all, an ephe-
meral thing. Given the complexities of international relations
as they are practiced by the human race, today's enemies may
well be tomorrow's friends.

This point was graphically illuminated to me immediately
following cessation of hostilities in World War II. I was in
Balikpapan, Borneo, at the time. The hatred of Australian
soldiers for the Japanese was proverbial there, yet that same
afternoon I saw Australian soldiers and Japanese prisoners
of war bouncing along in an American Jeep laughing and joking
as though they had been friends for years.

The second point I would have stressed, as I have hun-
dreds of times both in writing and speaking, is that "the
Chapel is dedicated to all Vietnam veterans: the living, the
dead, and the maimed in body and spirit." As the Disabled
American Veterans organization so well realizes, perhaps
the maimed in body and spirit are the most important of all,
for they must live—often agonizingly—with their afflictions. *
This understanding should not be demeaned one iota in any
sensitive mind by the fact that we memorialize the dead in
a special way by placing their photos in the Chapel, for nothing is as final as death.

My third emphasis would have been my answer when I
am asked why we built the Chapel. I reply, "We who <u>must</u>

---

*In 1977 the DAV made a grant to the Chapel of $10,000
a year for ten years.

will do what we <u>must</u> to encourage mankind to preserve rather
than to destroy." In this era when we are faced with the un-
deniable possibility of ultimate destruction by nuclear holo-
caust, I can see no possible value for mankind collectively
in harboring old enmities and hatreds that can only bespeak
the philosophy: "I am better than you." If, in the international arena, this boils down to a confrontation between na-
tionalism and internationalism, I must pick up the gauntlet
of the former and defend the latter. I would hope to do so
without being labeled unpatriotic, but I would do so none the
less.

Yet it is the scheme of things in life that there would be
others on the opposite side. While I would strive mightily
for my cause, I would hope to have the grace to extend the
hand of friendship to my opposition at the earliest possible
moment, and to continue to do so whenever a studied effort
would make it possible.

*        *        *

My mental behavioral patterns following David's death
may have seemed tinged with madness; nevertheless, they
set me on an unswerving, virtually single-minded and obses-
sive path toward the construction of the Vietnam Veterans
Memorial Chapel. Over the years that followed, whenever
my resolve weakened or I became weary of struggling with
apparently insurmountable obstacles, some mysterious dis-
closure always brought me back to my stubborn determination and lent me the mental, moral, and physical strength
to continue. What this power was I do not know, but it
seemed no less than the prompting of my son directed by
the hand of God watching patiently over my shoulder and
gently guiding me whenever I faltered. If this be madness,
I am content to have been mad.

During the years from 1968 to 1975 I finally learned an
important lesson from these dreams although, upon looking
back, it seems as though I was extremely slow in arriving
at the humility required to understand the true nature of my
role in relation to the Chapel. I was to be a vehicle for the
transmission of ideas and action into its construction.

It happened that the architect, Ted Luna, believed that
various foundations and trusts would fall all over each other
to lend financial support. Accordingly, from the fall of 1968
through the spring of 1969, I involved myself in the time con-

141

suming and laborious process of making requests for funding.
I learned that I was either not a good promoter, or else the
Chapel was not to be supported in this manner. All of my
time and effort was absolutely wasted.

Gradually, though, I learned that if I simply went to the
Chapel and worked with my own hands—and didn't expect too
much too soon—the funding came right there. I didn't have to
go out and beat the bushes for it, but I absolutely did have to
have faith. I doubt that I could have done so without these
sustaining and timely visions. For the most part I make no
attempt to explain their meaning, only to report them.

The first of these revealments occurred early on June 11,
1968, the morning after we returned to Val Verde from David's
funeral. When my relatives left later that morning I was con-
soling them instead of being consoled. My last words to them
before they left were: "I have everything under control." What
had given me the power to reverse the usual roles in this manner?

At six o'clock that morning a visiting friend, named Dale,
unbeknown to me arose and departed from the house. Guided
by a compelling impulse he walked up to the golf course accompanied by Bozo, a neighbor's Great Pyrenees dog who stopped by to visit us from time to time. There Dale was prompted
to sing aloud numerous patriotic songs such as "America the
Beautiful," while standing on a prominent feature of the terrain. A little later I broke away from my relatives and also
went up to the golf course. There I came out of the woods and
made the turn on to Bonito Lane. I was utterly unconscious of
what was to follow. I perceived nothing special until halfway
to Piño street when I encountered a blinding light such as one
might see when emerging from a tunnel. Along with the light
I saw David standing on the topmost point of the berm of No.
6 green in a characteristic attitude with his left hand on Bozo's
head.

Perhaps psychologists would say that I wanted to see
David and that it was Dale all along; nevertheless, I became
momentarily unconscious and David was no longer there. Instead I saw Dale. What is more, three times that night I
saw—not in my mind's eye,but engraved on the lids of my
closed eyes—the precise image. I concluded in a letter to
an uncle explaining this happening: "I have tried to see no
more; I am content."

*      *      *

By October 8, 1968, the Chapel construction was behind schedule and I was becoming increasingly agitated, but an occurrence of that date brought me back to an even keel. I explained in a letter to our youngest son, Douglas:

This morning just before I awakened at 5:45 (about the time David was killed allowing for time zone differental) I had a dream, or vision, or whatever it might be called. There was a general gathering of many people, David among them. I saw him standing beside you and beside Mother, but not beside you and Mother at the same time, nor do I recall any conversation with either of you. The only conversation I recall him participating in was with some unidentified person in which he was explaining the last thing that happened to him in Vietnam. He, David, was walking down a gulley or swale explaining (as it came to me, to one of his buddies) that he outranked him because he was a college graduate when (as it came to me) everything went "bla."

At the time I did not understand the significance of this dream in detail, but I was confident that I eventually would and this confidence buoyed up my spirits sufficiently so that I could diplomatically speed up the Chapel construction.

*　　　　*　　　　*

A corollary to this dream occurred on March 13, 1969, when my wife was visiting her sister in Albuquerque and I was alone at Val Verde. During the afternoon I became so disconsolate at the apparently insurmountable frustrations of building the Chapel that I wept uncontrollably for four hours. During this time I sorted lovingly through those of David's possessions that had been returned from Vietnam. As dusk approached I arose wearily and turned on a nearby three-stage light. I knew that the center stage of this light had been burned out for months, and I had to turn past this burned out portion to reach the brighter light. This time that center stage came on! Right then I knew that nothing could stop the Chapel effort.

And immediately I also realized that there must be thirteen photos of deceased Vietnam veterans in the Chapel, that the cross therein must be 13 feet high, and that we must fly a 13 star flag—the original flag of our nation. I was born on

143

October 13, 1913, and that number had repeatedly marked significant events in my life, but I did not right then understand its significance on this occasion.

Its importance was revealed to me on the last day of the following year when I learned from 1st Sergeant Tom McKinney that there were 13 killed from David's company in the engagement in which he lost his life—each from a different state. They were:

| | |
|---|---|
| Denver J. Berkheimer | Ohio |
| Roger Boyd | Illinois |
| Davis F. Brown | Florida |
| Alejandro Diaz | New York |
| William Hamacher | New Jersey |
| Clyde S. Hamby | California |
| Robert E. Harris | Kentucky |
| Rolando Hernandez | Texas |
| James R. Joshua | Alabama |
| Charles Kirkland | Missouri |
| Jerry A. Longtime | Minnesota |
| David Westphall | New Mexico |
| Ray Williams | Georgia |

At the same time I learned from Sergeant McKinney that Lance Corporal Charles Kirkland was both David's radio operator and special friend. Charles was the son of a minister from Kennett, Missouri. They were both killed at precisely the same instant. But a little earlier David had convinced Charles that he should go on to college and get his degree when he got out of the Marine Corps.

Was David's buddy whom I had dreamed about on October 8, 1968, Charles Kirkland? This seemed probable to me. Was David's pointing out that he was Charles' superior officer because he had a college degree analagous to persuading him to seek a degree? I believed that it was.

Another circumstance of the dream was fully as startling. In it I had also received the impression that this swale was in a clearing surrounded by dense growth, and so reported to many people. A letter from Sergeant McKinney of December 24, 1970, confirmed both the clearing and the swale; furthermore, that the surrounding dense growth was hedgerows. All of this was corroborated by Captain William Jason Spangler when I met him on the first day of 1971. Captain Spangler had assumed command of Bravo Company the day following the ambush.

144

*          *          *

In December 1968, I continued to make applications for grants of money from various foundations to complete the Chapel, and encountered only negative reactions. I had expected more positive results and was terribly depressed. I needed a boost in my morale, which came on the morning of December 9. I reported to Douglas in a letter:

> This morning just prior to 6:00 A.M. I awoke with the following vividly in my mind. I had just received (or at least had in my hands) a letter of many pages (perhaps 20) on light blue paper somewhat longer and narrower than letter size. A date was in the upper right hand corner, but I do not know what date it was. The letter was in three folds and the writing did not start until near the bottom most of the three folds. There seemed to be no address—the letter just started. I have no recollection of removing the letter from the envelope. It was, somehow, just in my hands and I had started to read. I remember glancing at the second page and on it the writing started near the top of the page. I remember the words "Major MacLean" and "Inquiry why one of my men was killed by the NVA." Then I noticed that the ink was running. I was frantically casting about in my mind for something to stop the ink from running when I awakened.

Lieutenant Colonel J.H. MacLean, David's newly appointed battalion commander had written to us explaining the circumstance of David's death, but I did not attach any particular significance to his letter in relation to this dream. More important to me was a conception that I conveyed to Douglas at the time:

> Now I know that visions are not considered a valid part of the historical process in ascertaining truth, but I am not against these things leading to more tangible facets of knowledge or tying in with what I know from more tangible sources. What the outcome will be, I do not know, but I am learning to neither fight nor force the issues involved. I do know that they give me an inner peace, and possibly that is all that is involved. But I feel that it goes deeper than that, possibly much deeper. We will just have to wait and see.

*　　　　*　　　　*

We knew that David was a talented writer, but he was
never satisfied with much that he wrote, particularly his poetry, and destroyed a great deal before he left for Vietnam.  As
a consequence, we were particularly hopeful that there might
be some of his writings in his personal belongings that were
to be returned from Vietnam.  It was a low day in our lives
when the boxes finally arrived and I opened them.  There were
no personal items whatever—nothing of his writings or correspondence—only clothing and such.

I was finally relieved from this heavy burden in an unusual
way.  On the morning of January 20, 1969, as I awakened I had
a mental image of a wooden box, related to David, and valued
at $2145.01 and labeled G-19.  This message was meaningless
to me at the time, but I sent it on to Douglas who was then a
captain in the Air Force.  He recalled that a certain Air Force
map was labeled G-19, and sent me a copy.  I carefully examined it and learned that the stated dollar value proved to
be the coordinates at the location of Wheeler Peak.  Before he
left for Vietnam, David had crossed the tangled wilderness
from our home to that location to test his mettle as a combat
marine.

I set down my reaction in a letter to Douglas dated February 6, 1969:

> The information that you conveyed regarding the map
> and the coordinates staggers and humbles me.  To me it
> can only mean that David's possessions are irretrievably
> lost; and that we should no longer bother ourselves in the
> matter.  I am relieved and I am content.

*　　　　*　　　　*

On August 24, 1969, I further explained to Douglas my feelings concerning these periodic revelations:

> The periods before these five A.M. enlightenments
> are not easy for me, Doug, but I can bear them, not easily,
> but bear them, as long as I retain my confidence that they
> are a part of the chapel building process.  Perhaps the har-
> dest part is keeping these things quite much to myself, but
> I know now that I must do so.  Finishing the chapel may
> not be easy, and it might take longer than we might wish,

146

but it will be done.

Still, my special unease continued for the next 10 days.
Every night just before I went to sleep, yet while still perfectly conscious, something in my subconscious mind was transported to David's casket in the National Cemetery at Santa
Fe and was called upon to view his remains therein, but each
time I fearfully held back. Finally on the morning of September
3, it came to me that what I was really being called upon to do
was to go to the trunk and measure the size of his photo therein, because I needed these dimensions in order to write a letter to Ho Chi Minh, President of North Vietnam:

> While your country and mine are at war, if the lessons of
> history are a valid indication, they will not always be so.
> We have lost a son in that war. As a result of that loss,
> and as a testimonial of faith in the ultimate goodness
> of man, we are building the Vietnam Veterans Peace and
> Brotherhood Chapel.

> Photos of deceased veterans of the war in Vietnam will be
> therein presented to view, and they will be changed each
> month. Also on view will be two inscriptions—enclosed—
> from the writings of our son.

> We invite your people to send photos of their deceased
> veterans. If at all possible they should be in color, and
> they must be eight inches by ten inches in size.

Before I mailed these letters I learned that Ho Chi Minh
had just died, but I mailed them anyway.

*     *     *

On September 10, H.W. Potter wrote a letter to me that resulted in the first national publicity for the Chapel. "Red"
Potter is a retired newspaper man of Taos, New Mexico,
and was engaged in free-lance writing of feature articles for
newspapers. He and his wife, Pat, had visited the Chapel
which then consisted of only the block walls. I had left a
brief statement, along with my name and address, framed
upon the bare block walls. His letter followed. He propheti-
cally wrote in part:

I am engaged in free-lance writing of feature articles for magazines and it occurred to me that such exposure might result in financial support from unexpected sources and perhaps speed completion of your project.

As a result of Mr. Potter's efforts, aided by Mr. Wylie Stewart, a retired Scripps-Howard newspaper executive, a nationally syndicated "Newspaper Enterprises Association" article about the Chapel appeared on March 30, 1970, and was reprinted in numerous newspapers througout the United States as well as in "Pacific Stars and Stripes." There followed numerous inquiries from widely scattered interested persons, as well as several small donations for construction of the Chapel. This publicity encouraged me to construct a sign located at the highway and an outdoor visitors center nearby incorporating a model as it would appear when completed as well as a brief statement about the Chapel.

*   *   *

In the aggregate, work on the Chapel was exasperatingly slow. Despite everything I could do personally, another winter was approaching with still a great deal of work yet remaining. As the days and months lengthened into years, it would have been abnormal not to have had periods of discouragement. Once again I was bolstered by an unforgetable happening. On the morning of September 24, I awakened at my usual time of shortly after five, then inexplicably dozed off again. At 6:45 I awakened suddenly and fully with the following account vividly in mind:

 I was attending a fund raising in a certain room (a fund raising for the Chapel?). I had on a long coat and a belt (my Navy overcoat?). In the room was a crippled boy in his very early teens perhaps thirteen, who had no use of his legs. In the room was a barbell lying on the floor. Suddenly the crippled boy had hold of the handle of the barbell with his arms straight out in front, his body rigid, and his feet dragging behind. He remained in this position while the barbell dragged him out of the room, across a road, up an earthen enbankment, and into the entrance of a building. While I have only a fleeting recollection of this entrance, it was not unlike the entrance to the Chapel. I ran desperatly behind the crippled boy

148

and crossed the threshold into a room. In it was a row of tables made from crude planks. In due course the people who were with us in the first room assembled in the second room with the crippled boy and myself. The music of bells had started to play when the crippled boy left the room pulled by his barbell and continued until all were assembled in the second room.

The people started in a desultory fashion to lay, small amounts of money on the tables (for the chapel?). Suddenly, and spontaneously, there came from their pockets a flood of bills of large denomination FOR THE CRIPPLED BOY!

What did I make of this when I awakened? I now realize that the Chapel effort had to be centered in myself. My family and many others have helped; even so, as meritorious as the idea of the Chapel was in itself, it apparently was destined to be looked upon with apathy by a generation of Americans who wanted to forget the war in Vietnam. What was needed was a catalyst, a story of one man who would not, could not, forget. This made news. I did not actively seek that role, nor did I back away from it. I was willing to serve in any honorable role that would advance the prosperity of the Vietnam Veterans Memorial Chapel and Center for the Advancement of Human Dignity.

*   *   *

On January 7, 1971, I again dreamed about David. Earlier ones had always been between the hours of five and six in the morning. This time, however, I awakened at 1:13 A.M. and immediately wrote down my impression:

I just had a dream about Dave. We were in a barn together and a fire started. The fire was licking its way with red, angry flames up one of the supporting posts of the barn. Dave was putting out the fire with his bare hands while I went for a bucket of water. By the time I got there with the water he had the flames essentially out, but I threw the water on the fire to put out the last embers. Then I took David's hands in mine and said, "You didn't have to do it that way." There were holes burned in his hands and I was holding them in mine and kissing them so they wouldn't hurt so much when I woke up.

I don't know what this means, but. . .

I still don't know what this means, but I might have some ideas when I escape to that unassailable fortress of my own mind where I alone can retreat unless I invite another to accompany me. But I will cheerfully allow others to have equal latitude with my own in examining the enchantment of that moment.

*   *   *

Occasionally there were episodes other than dreams related to David that kept me on an even keel. More often than not these came in the fall when winter was about to close in and mark the end of another year's work on the Chapel with the completion still not in sight. One of these occurred on October 15, 1971. I had just installed the glass entrance door. Even though the interior was still unfinished, from habit I kept it locked. Even then, however, the majestic architectural lines of the building's exterior were an invitation for sensitive persons to enter. One morning I returned and found a crudely lettered sign on a piece of scrap plywood that asked the question: "Why did you lock me out when I needed to come in?"

*   *   *

By early in 1975 the Chapel still had problems, but had created enough national impact so that bills were introduced in both the United States Senate and House to make the Chapel a national monument. While no legislation resulted, it now seemed certain that the Chapel effort could not die.

Perhaps this is why on Sunday, September 21, 1975, David apparently signed off. In some ways, I suppose, this last message was the most unusual of all. I awoke at 4:00 A.M. with my teeth aching violently, so took a swallow of wine and tried to relax. I went back to sleep and awakened at about 6:30 with my teeth feeling as though the pain were masked.

I had just been with David. I was seated on the edge of the bed at the Chapel office and he was sitting in a chair opposite from me. He was playing his guitar, a fantastic instrument with unusual features including a delicate chain that hung over the strings to mute them in a certain way. Another innovation was a system of buttons that, when pressed, evidently changed the chording arrangement in a subtle way. I

150

asked him about these buttons and he started to speak, but only an unclear sound resulted. Then, as though realizing the sound was discordant relative to the delicate-clarity of the guitar music and might set my teeth to resume violent aching, he audibly, clearly, delicately, and shyly uttered the single word: "Oops." I impulsively reached out to touch him with a gesture of compassionate understanding, but he was gone and I was awake.

Significantly, in his youth David had picked up a habit of asking questions with a falling inflection. He eventually overcame this mannerism; nevertheless, many times before he did so—when he lapsed into the old style—he had uttered to me this single word: "Oops."

Was this reminder that he had once broken a certain habit an indication to me that I was now on my own in carrying on the Chapel work—that I could no longer count on the support of his periodic visitations? I do not know, but I do know that he did not come again. Over the years since then I have been depressed at times, but I have never lost faith in the Chapel effort. Even now I know that David would sign on again if he were ever needed.